The Bible from Alef to Tav

Penina V. Adelman

artwork by Michael Jacobs

Torah Aura Productions

ISBN# 0-933873-22-0

Copyright © 1998 Penina V. Adelman

Color Illustrations Copyright © 1998 Michael Jacobs

Published by Torah Aura Productions

Torah Aura Productions • 4423 Fruitland Avenue, Los Angeles, CA 90058
(800) 238–6724 • (323) 585-7312 • fax (323) 585–0327 • e-mail <misrad@torahaura.com>
Visit the Torah Aura Website at WWW.TORAHAURA.COM

MANUFACTURED IN THE UNITED STATES OF AMERICA

For Daniel, Laura and Gil
who wanted a book of their own
while the grown-ups read Torah;
and for Steve
עֵזֶר כְּנֶגְדִּי/ezer k'negdi/
my helpmate.

How I Came to Write
The Bible from Alef to Tav

In the early '90s when my eldest son Daniel was able to sit with me in synagogue, I used to lean over to him and whisper in his ear a sort of simultaneous translation of the Torah portion into words he could understand. This was all right for awhile until the day he complained, "Mommy, why can't I have my own book now?"

I began thinking about what such a book would look like. Of course it would have plenty of illustrations, and the stories would be told in plain, simple English. There was nothing like this in our local Jewish bookstore or in the town library. Thus, the idea for a new children's Bible was hatched.

Children often learn right alongside their parents, and the reverse is true, too, especially today when many children are becoming literate in Bible and Jewish practice before their parents. So the book evolved into a way for children and adults to learn Bible stories and the letters of the Hebrew Alef-Bet together.

Daniel and Laura, my two older children are past needing such a book now. However, their litter brother Gil, who is three years old, will be just the right age to bring *The Bible from Alef to Tav* with him so he can read along when the grownups are reading the Torah portion.

May this Bible bring the teachings of the Hebrew Bible and the wisdom of the Hebrew Alef-Bet to all those who want to learn.

Penina V. Adelman
10th of Tammuz 5758
July 4, 1998
Newtonville, Massachusetts

Thanks

There are many people I'd like to thank, but the following people and institutions deserve to be singled out: my mother, Selma Williams, who has taught me much of what I know about writing; my father, Burt Williams, who gave me advice at many critical points in the process; Pardes Institute of Jewish Studies in Jerusalem, which nurtured my love of Torah; Rabbi Sue Levi Elwell and Rabbi Ruth Sohn, who critiqued the manuscript in it early stages; the Torah study group I ran for Ethiopian women in Beer-Sheva who were feeling that they had already fallen so far behind their children since they had arrived in Israel, especially my co-workers Yaffa Yeshayahu and Kessaye Tevajieh.

Table of Contents

אֱלֹהִים ELOHIM [GOD]

אָדָם ADAM [ADAM]

אֲדָמָה ADAMAH [EARTH, GROUND]

According to Alef

א is the first letter of the Hebrew alphabet. In Hebrew the word for "alphabet" is alef-bet. Words can be relatives just like people. The Hebrew word "alef-bet" is the great-great-great-great-great grandparent of the English word "alphabet."

The letter א doesn't make a sound.

א is quiet: like you when you're sleeping, like your neighborhood just after the snow has fallen, like a valley in the desert in the hot afternoon, when nothing is moving or making any noise, no plants, no animals, no people.

Sh-sh-sh-sh-sh-sh-sh. Listen.

Can you hear your breathing?

The Creation of Adam

 When the world began, God breathed over the waters. God has many names. One name begins with a breath. One name of God begins with the letter אֱ.

אֱלֹהִים Elohim starts with אֱ.

אֱלֹהִים made the heavens and the earth.

אֱלֹהִים made אָדָם Adam (Adam).

אָדָם was the first human being.

אָדָם Adam

was born from the אֲדָמָה adamah (earth).

Elohim took a fistful of earth
and shaped it into Adam.
The letters that spell אָדָם Adam
come from אֲדָמָה adamah, too.

Listen.
Can you hear how adamah comes from Adam?
Adam, adamah, אֲדָמָה, אָדָם.

When אֱלֹהִים Elohim breathed into Adam's nostrils,
אָדָם Adam started breathing, too, and came alive.
אָדָם Adam changed from one person into two.
The original אָדָם
split into the first man and the first woman.

In the beginning, all things came from Elohim.
And אֱלֹהִים begins with the letter א.

ACTIVITIES

1. *To think about*: When do you like to be quiet? When do you like to be noisy?

2. What things in the world are very quiet? What things are very noisy? Imitate some of these things.

3. Can you "say something" without words, using your body and your voice?

4. Draw a picture of the first human beings—the first man and the first woman.

Chapter Two: BET

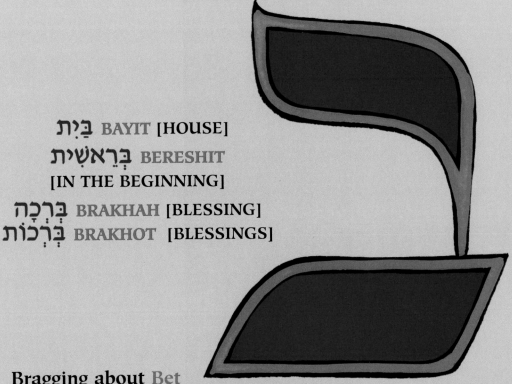

בַּיִת BAYIT [HOUSE]
בְּרֵאשִׁית BERESHIT
[IN THE BEGINNING]
בְּרָכָה BRAKHAH [BLESSING]
בְּרָכוֹת BRAKHOT [BLESSINGS]

Bragging about Bet

בּ Bet is the second letter of the alef-bet, and it sounds like the letter "B." It is also a word that means "house" or בַּיִת bayit. Can you see a house in the letter בּ?

בּ is the kind of house where the front door is always open so that all the words and stories of the Torah can come out and step right onto these pages where you can read them.

בּ begins the word that begins the Torah, בְּרֵאשִׁית Bereshit. It means "Beginning." The very first story in the Torah is the story of the beginning of the world.

When you were born, that was your beginning. When the world was born, that was another kind of beginning. Come inside the door of בּ, find a cozy chair or lap to sit on, and listen to what happened...

The Six Days of Beginning

בְּרֵאשִׁית Bereshit: The Beginning.

 On the first day,
אֱלֹהִים Elohim created
light from the darkness
so we could see.

 On the second day,
אֱלֹהִים Elohim made
heaven up above
so the sun, moon, and stars
would have a place to live.

 On the third day,
אֱלֹהִים Elohim made
all the things that grow from little seeds
and give us their fruits and vegetables
to eat: the grasses that give us wheat,
barley, and rye to make the flour
that we use in breads and cakes;
the plants that give us peas, beans,
peppers, grapes, and strawberries
to use in salad and fruit cups;
the trees that give us figs, almonds,
and apples to eat and enjoy.
Can you name some more fruits and
vegetables that you like to eat?

 On the fourth day,
אֱלֹהִים Elohim made
the sun, moon, and stars
to light up the sky by day and night.

On the fifth day,
אֱלֹהִים Elohim made
the fish to swim in the waters
and the birds to fly in the air.

On the sixth day,
אֱלֹהִים Elohim made
the animals that creep and crawl
on the earth.

אֱלֹהִים Elohim also made
Adam and Eve,
the first people to live on the earth
along with all other living things.

Together the first people,
the first plants and trees,
the first fish
and birds
and animals
learned how to feed
and take care of one another
so they could all keep
growing
on the earth forever.

On the seventh day,
the world was all done.
Elohim stopped making things.
Elohim took the time
to give a בְּרָכָה brakhah (blessing)
for the seventh day.

A בְּרָכָה is a way of giving thanks
for something wonderful.
In Hebrew, each בְּרָכָה starts with
בָּרוּךְ אַתָּה יְיָ "Barukh Attah Adonai"
(Blessed are you, God...).

This day
that Elohim blessed
is called Shabbat,
the day of rest.

Shabbat feels
like a בְּרָכָה brakhah,
like a quiet and peaceful בַּיִת bayit (house).

Shabbat is like
a בַּיִת that you can go and live in
at the end of every week.

People started copying Elohim,
resting on the seventh day, too.

When you enter the bayit of Shabbat,
you stop doing the things
and making the things
you do all the other days of the week.
You just feel the beauty of this world
that Elohim has made.
You take a walk in the woods,
or read a book,
or eat a delicious, yummy meal
with your family and friends.

These are the בְּרָכוֹת brakhot
of the day of rest.

ACTIVITIES

1. Draw a picture of the Creation of the world.

2. Dance the Creation of the world using movement and gestures to convey what happened on each of the seven days.

3. Have you ever made something "from scratch" with your mother or father, with a friend, grandparent, or teacher? What did you do? Think of a project you could do together: cooking something, planting seeds, weaving or sewing, building something.

4. Think of something in your neighborhood that needs to be cleaned up, a stream, hillside, woods. Make it look like it was "just created" again. Renewal is part of Creation.

5. Go outside and see how many things you can bless. Practice saying brakhot (blessings) together and make up some of your own.

6. Draw the letters alef and bet. Do the shapes of the letters remind you of something? Go ahead and draw whatever these letters bring to mind.

Chapter Three: GIMMEL

גָּמָל GAMAL [CAMEL]

גֶּשֶׁם GESHEM [RAIN]

Glowing about Gimmel

ג Gimmel is a letter that sounds a lot like the name of a desert animal. For many days at a time this animal can go without water, which helps if you live in the dry, dusty desert.

גָּמָל Gamal is the Hebrew name of this animal. Can you guess what it is? It's a camel.

ג Gimmel, גָּמָל Gamal, camel.

Camel. גָּמָל Gamal ג Gimmel.

When you say these three words, you can hear that they sound just like three cousins from the same family.

Noah's Ark

Once there was a family
that loved the earth
and all the animals on it
very much.
This family lived
a long, long time after אָדָם Adam (Adam).
They remembered how אָדָם Adam
was born from אֲדָמָה adamah, the Earth.

One day Noah, the father,
heard אֱלֹהִים Elohim say,

"NOAH,

THIS WORLD HAS BECOME FULL OF MEAN PEOPLE

DOING MEAN THINGS.

IT CANNOT GO ON THIS WAY.

I HAVE DECIDED TO DESTROY ALL THAT LIVES HERE

EXCEPT FOR YOU AND YOUR FAMILY.

YOU ARE GOOD ENOUGH

AND KIND ENOUGH

TO HELP ME BUILD A BETTER WORLD.

"HERE IS WHAT YOU MUST DO.
BUILD AN ARK OUT OF WOOD.
THEN BRING TWO OF EVERY KIND OF ANIMAL,
MALE AND FEMALE, ONTO THE ARK.
YOU MUST BRING THE ONES THAT FLY.
YOU MUST BRING THE ONES THAT CREEP.
YOU MUST BRING THE ONES THAT WALK."

So Noa<u>h</u> built an ark.
There was enough room in it
for all the animals of the earth
and his family
to live together.
He did what
Elohim had told him to do.
He brought two of each animal
along with his family
to live in the ark.

As soon as everyone was in the ark,
the skies opened up.
Out poured גֶּשֶׁם geshem (rain).
The word גֶּשֶׁם sounds like falling rain.

Listen...
g-sh-sh-sh-mm-mm-mm;
g-sh-sh-sh-mm-mm-mm;
g-sh-sh-sh-mm-mm-mm.

גֶּשֶׁם kept coming for 40 days and 40 nights.
גֶּשֶׁם flooded over the villages,
trees and mountains.
The world was gone,
and there was only a deep, deep ocean.

No<u>a</u>h and his family wondered
if they would ever be able to go home again.

Suddenly one day
the geshem stopped.
The waters
that hid the land
began to dry up.
No<u>a</u>h sent
a dove out from the ark.
The dove came back
with an olive branch
in its beak.

Noah and his family jumped for joy
because the dove must have found a tree
on dry land.
Perhaps at last they could go back home.

אֱלֹהִים Elohim told Noah and his family,

"TAKE ALL THE ANIMALS WITH YOU
AND GO LIVE AGAIN ON THE EARTH.
BRING HER BACK TO LIFE AGAIN
BY TREATING HER LIKE ONE OF YOUR FAMILY.

"SEE THIS BOW,
THAT I AM PUTTING
IN THIS CLOUD.
WHEN YOU SEE MY BOW
AFTER A RAINSTORM,
LET ALL THE COLORS
REMIND YOU
HOW MUCH I LOVE YOU
AND THE EARTH.

"LET THE RAINBOW REMIND YOU
THAT ALL WHO LIVE ON THE EARTH
ARE PART OF ONE BIG FAMILY.
YOU MUST TAKE CARE OF YOUR FAMILY
AND THE GOOD RED EARTH THAT IS YOUR HOME.

"IF YOU DO THIS,
I SHALL NEVER AGAIN DESTROY
ALL THAT LIVES ON THE EARTH:
THE ORANGE ORANGES,
THE YELLOW CORN,
THE GREEN LEAVES,
THE BLUE SEAS,
THE PURPLE VIOLETS,
THE BLACK SPIDERS,
THE BROWN WHEAT,
THE WHITE SHEEP.

"FROM NOW ON,
AFTER גֶּשֶׁם
COMES THE RAINBOW,
AND AFTER THE RAINBOW
COMES NEW LIFE."

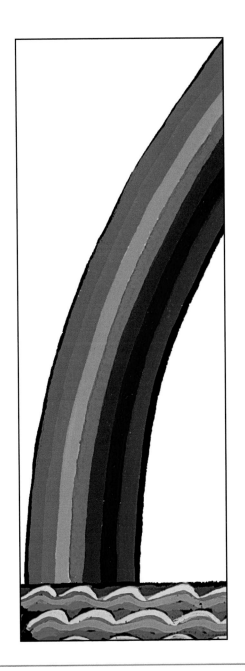

ACTIVITIES

1. *To think about*: Imagine that you were an animal on the ark. What would your life be like for those 40 days and nights?

2. Name animals, plants, flowers, insects, and other things in nature for every color of the rainbow.

3. Sing songs about Noah's ark, rainbows, colors.

Chapter Four: DALET

דֶּלֶת DELET [DOOR]

דְּבָרִים D'VARIM
[WORDS, THINGS]

Discovering Dalet

Come right inside the door of ד Dalet and see what you can find.
ד is a very kind letter, welcoming you to come in, sit down, and
have something to eat and drink. ד likes visitors anytime. In
Hebrew the word for door is דֶּלֶת delet, which sounds like ד.

Can you see a door in the letter ד? In Hebrew, each letter is a
doorway to a world. Sometimes words have worlds inside them.
When you hear the word "circus," can you smell the peanuts and
cotton candy? Can you hear the ringmaster's loud voice and a
clown blowing a horn? Can you see the trapeze artist swinging
higher and higher in her glittering costume? All this comes into
your head just from one word, "circus." Words can make worlds.

Abraham, Sarah, and the Three Guests

Abraham and Sarah
learned a lot from the letter ד dalet.
They learned about welcoming guests
into their home.

Abraham and Sarah
were a husband and wife from long ago.
They lived in a tent in the hot, dry desert.
This is the way many people in the Bible
used to live.

Abraham and Sarah did not have a car.
They did not have a telephone.
They did not have a bathtub.
They did not have a refrigerator.
They did not have running water.

Instead, they had each other for company.
They had camels to ride on.
They had a tent for shelter
from the sun and wind.

But, they did not have a child.
That was the one thing they really wanted.

In those days,
if somebody came to your tent,
you invited them in.
That was the rule of the desert.
Sarah and Abraham always
followed this rule.
They really enjoyed
opening their דֶּלֶת delet (door)
to others.

Once Abraham was sitting in the דֶּלֶת
of his tent at the hottest time of the day.
He looked out into the desert
and saw three people coming.
He was so happy
to be able to help anyone
who was hot and tired.
He ran to greet them.

Abraham asked the three to come into his tent
to rest and have some food and drink.
He said to Sarah,
"Please make some cakes for our guests."

Sarah went right away
to make her special cakes.
Abraham brought water
to wash the hot, dusty feet of the strangers.
They had been walking
for a very long time through the desert.

The strangers thanked Abraham and Sarah
for their kindness.
Then one of them said,
"Next year when I come back this way,
you will have a son."

Sarah laughed
when she heard
these דְּבָרִים d'varim (words).

She said,

"BUT I AM OLD,
TOO OLD TO GIVE BIRTH TO A CHILD.
HOW CAN THIS COME TO BE?"

The visitor said,
"IS ANYTHING TOO HARD FOR GOD TO DO?
YOU WILL SEE,
NEXT YEAR AT THIS TIME
YOU WILL HAVE A SON!"

These wonderful דְּבָרִים d'varim came true.
Next year when their son was born
Abraham and Sarah were very happy.
They called him Isaac, which means Laughter.
This reminded them
of how Sarah had laughed
as she stood at the דֶּלֶת delet of the tent
and heard the news that she would give birth.
Abraham and Sarah
taught their son to keep his דֶּלֶת
open to strangers at all times.
They taught him to help

those who were far from their homes
and far from their families.
This is the way of the desert,
the way of the Jewish People.

ACTIVITIESyone whose home you like to visit, who is as
generous and welcoming as Abraham and Sarah? What do you do when
guests come to visit your home?

2. Draw a picture or make a model of life in the desert. The Bedouins who live
in Israel today have a lifestyle that is quite similar to that of Abraham and
Sarah.

Chapter Five: HEH

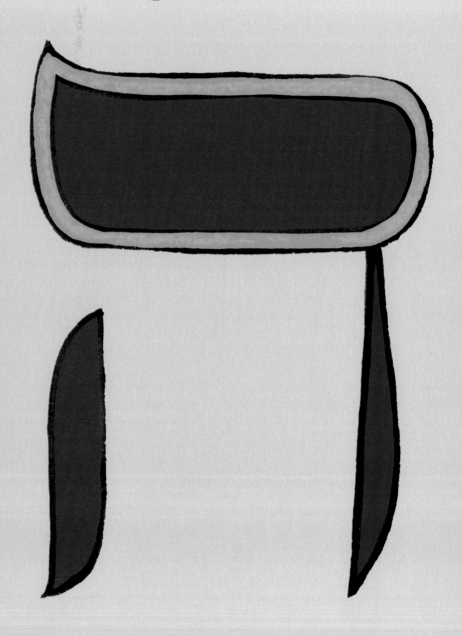

הַלְלוּיָה HALLELUJAH [PRAISE GOD]

הַיּוֹם HA-YOM [TODAY]

Hearing the Heh

Here is the letter ה heh. How do you know a ה heh when you hear one? ה Heh sounds like "H" in the English alphabet. Go ahead, make a ה heh sound. Take a deep breath in through your nose. Now, breathe out through your mouth, Hah-ah-ah-ah-ah...

Wind blowing through pine trees at night or a big seashell you hold up to your ear make the sound of ה heh. Can you see how ה heh makes room for air to blow right through it?

ה Heh, the Helper

ה Heh is a good helper. A heh at the beginning of a word helps you know that this is not just any old something, but a very special something. גָּמָל Gamal means a camel, any camel you see trudging along in the desert. הַגָּמָל ha-Gamal means the camel, the one you saw today standing under a palm tree, drinking.

A ה heh at the end of a name helps you know that this is the name of a girl or a woman. Sarah, Rebeccah, Leah, Hannah—all these are the names of women in the Torah, and all end with ה heh.

Rebekkah at the Well

Here is the story of Rebekkah,
a helpful girl with a good heart.

Do you remember
Abraham and Sarah,
how kind they were to guests?
Because of their kindness,
they heard that soon they would have a baby
after waiting so many years.

The baby's name was Isaac.
Abraham and Sarah loved him very much.
When Sarah died,
Abraham decided that it was time
for Isaac to be married.

In those days,
young men and women did not choose
the one they would marry
the way they do הַיּוֹם ha-yom (today).
Instead, the parents of the man
talked with the parents of the woman
about getting their children married
and joining the two families together.

That is why
Abraham sent
his servant, Eliezer,
to find
a good woman
to be Isaac's wife.

Eliezer took ten camels with him
and went to the city of Nahor.
He was very thirsty from traveling in the desert,
so he went right to the well.
There, as he stopped to let the camels rest,
he prayed,

"OH, GOD,
PLEASE HELP ME FIND A WIFE FOR ISAAC.
WHEN THE YOUNG WOMEN AND GIRLS
COME TO THIS WELL TO DRAW WATER
THIS EVENING,
I SHALL ASK EACH ONE FOR A DRINK
FROM HER PITCHER.
THE ONE WHO ANSWERS,
'PLEASE DRINK,
AND I SHALL GIVE YOUR CAMELS WATER ALSO,'
SHE WILL BE THE ONE
YOU HAVE CHOSEN FOR ISAAC."

Even as Eliezer was finishing his prayer,
Rebekkah was walking to the well
with a pitcher on her shoulder.
Eliezer ran to her and asked,
"Please, could I have a little water
from your pitcher?"

"Of course you may, sir," said Rebekkah.

As soon as he had drunk his fill,
Rebekkah said,

"I shall also give your camels water to drink.
It is so hot הַיּוֹם ha-yom (today).
They must be very thirsty, too."

Now Eliezer was sure
that this was the wife for Isaac,
because she was so kind and thoughtful.
He said, "הַלְלוּיָה Halleluyah!
Praise God who has helped me find
a wife for my master's son!"

Eliezer gave Rebekkah
an earring
and two bracelets of gold.
They made her
even more beautiful
than she was already.
Then he asked to speak
with her parents.

He told them,
"הַיּוֹם Ha-yom (Today)
your daughter, Rebekkah,
has been very kind to me.

She has given water to me,
and to my camels as well.
This is a sign from God
that she is to marry my master's son.
Will you let Rebekkah come with me?"

Rebekkah's parents asked her
if she wished to go and marry Isaac.

"Yes, I do," she answered.

"הַלְלוּיָהּ Halleluyah (Praise God)!"
shouted Eliezer.

This is how Rebekkah
came to live in the house of Abraham,
where she married Isaac.
She became one of the great Mothers of Israel.

ACTIVITIES

1. *To think about*: In ancient times, the well was the place where people came to meet each other. Name some "wells" today.

2. What is a family tree? Here is the family tree of Isaac and Rebekkah.

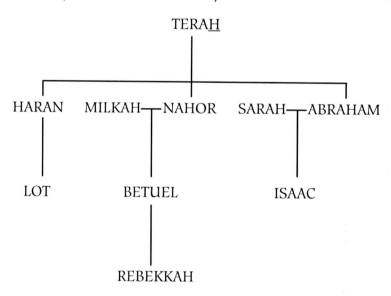

What does your family tree look like?

3. *The Fathers and the Mothers*: The Jewish People have seven ancestors who are called the Fathers (Patriarchs) and the Mothers (Matriarchs). These are the great-great-great-great-great-great (and many more greats) grandparents of the Jewish People. Draw pictures for your Torah family album of the Fathers and Mothers you have heard about so far: Abraham and Sarah, Isaac and Rebekkah.

Chapter Six: VAV

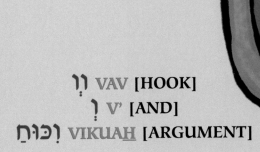

וָו VAV [HOOK]
וְ V' [AND]
וִכּוּחַ VIKUAH [ARGUMENT]

Visiting with וָו Vav

Very few letters appear as often as וָו vav. The word וָו vav means "hook" in Hebrew. וָו Vav hooks words together like this:

Adam וְ v'adamah (Adam and the Earth); Moshe וְ v' Miriam (Moses and Miriam); Ya'akov וְ v'Esau (Jacob and Esau). In Hebrew, the "V" sound means "and."

Can you say V-V-V-V-V-V-? Very, very good! The sound of the English letter "V" makes the same sound as the וָו vav in Hebrew. Now you can see what a valuable letter וָו vav is.

Jacob and Esau

Rebekkah וְ (and) Isaac
wanted children very much.

Isaac prayed to God,
and soon Rebekkah
was pregnant with twins.

The two baby boys fought
even before they were born.
They were still inside their mother.
Rebekkah could feel them fighting inside her.

She asked God,
"Why are my babies fighting already?"

God answered,
"You are going to give birth to
two different peoples.
One will be stronger than the other,
and the older one
will bow down to the younger one."

What God said came true.

Esau was born first,
וְ V' Jacob was born second.
They were always fighting,
always having a וִכּוּחַ vikuah (argument).

In those days,
the father would give a special blessing
to the first-born child.
This blessing made this child feel very special.

As they grew up, the twins were very different.
Esau liked to hunt outdoors,
וְ Jacob liked to stay in the tent
to dream and think.

One day, Esau came in.
He was very tired and hungry.
Jacob was cooking lentil stew
that smelled delicious.
Esau said,
"Give me some of that stew.
I'm so hungry
I could eat a camel!"

Jacob replied,
"Promise you'll give me your birthright."

Esau said, "I promise.
What do I care about a birthright
when I'm about to die of hunger?"

So Jacob fed Esau some bread and lentil stew.
In return, Esau gave his birthright to Jacob.

This was not the only thing Esau gave up.
When their father, Isaac, was old and blind,
Jacob tricked him
into giving him Esau's blessing.
This was the blessing of the first-born.

Rebekkah helped Jacob
put goatskins on his arms.
When Isaac touched him,
he would feel hairy like Esau.
Rebekkah also prepared
Isaac's favorite food
just the way Esau made it.
In this way, Isaac was fooled
into blessing Jacob with the blessing
meant for his first-born son, Esau.

"SEE, THE SMELL OF MY SON
IS LIKE THE SMELL OF A FIELD GOD HAS BLESSED.
MAY GOD GIVE YOU
FROM THE DEW OF THE HEAVENS
AND FROM THE FRUITS OF THE EARTH....
MAY PEOPLES SERVE YOU
AND NATIONS BOW DOWN TO YOU.
MAY THOSE WHO CURSE YOU BE CURSED,
AND MAY THOSE WHO BLESS YOU BE BLESSED."

As soon as Isaac
was finished blessing Jacob,
Esau came in from hunting.

"Here is the meat you asked for,
Father.
Now give me your blessing,
please."

Then Isaac was confused and asked,
"But who was that? I just blessed *him!*"

Esau began to cry,
"But Father,
don't you have any more blessings for me?"

Isaac replied,
"YOU WILL LIVE ON THE EARTH'S FRUITS
AND THE HEAVENS' DEW.
YOU WILL LIVE BY YOUR SWORD,
AND YOU WILL SERVE YOUR BROTHER
UNTIL YOU BECOME STRONG ENOUGH
TO BE FREE OF HIM."

Even this blessing could not stop Esau
from being very, very angry with Jacob.
Esau was so angry he promised himself
that someday he would get back at his brother.

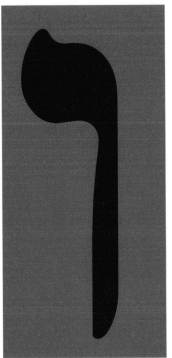

Jacob וְV'Esau.
Twin brothers.
Hooked together like a וָו vav.
Always trying
to get away from each other,
always coming back together,
always struggling,
always brothers.

ACTIVITIES

1. *To think about*: If you have a brother or a sister, can you think of a time when you felt jealous of him or her? What did you do or say? If you do not have a brother or sister, perhaps the adult you are reading this with does have one and can remember a time of jealousy and fighting. What could you have done differently in that situation? Act it out.

2. *Cook and aat*: Recipe for Esau's Lentil Stew

1 medium onion, chopped	1/8 t. cumin
1 large tomato, chopped	4 C. tomato soup
4 T. butter, margarine or oil	1 1/2 C. dried red lentils
1/4 t. turmeric	salt to taste
3 eggs	1/4 t. pepper
toasted pita	

   Sauté onion and tomato in oil. Add spices. Add tomato soup. Bring to a boil. Add lentils and simmer for 15 minutes. Break eggs into soup and stir. Serve with toasted pita. (From Daniel Cutler, *The Bible Cookbook*. New York: William Morrow & Co., 1985)

3. *A similar tale*: All over the world, stories about jealousy and rivalry between siblings abound. *Cinderella* and *Beauty and the Beast* are but two examples of such tales. Can you think of some more?

Chapter Seven: ZAYIN

זַיִן ZAYIN [WEAPON]
זֶרַע ZERA [SEED]

Zooming toward זַיִן Zayin

Imagine a zoo with zero animals. Instead of animals, this zoo is full of all kinds of wild letters in cages. What sound would the letter ז zayin make?

Say it out loud— ז zayin, ז zayin, ז zayin. Here's a hint—a bumblebee makes the same sound. That's right—z-z-z-z-z-z-z-z. ז zayin sounds just like the letter "Z."

The word זַיִן zayin in Hebrew means a weapon like a sword or a gun. Can you see a weapon in the shape of the letter ז zayin? Trace it with your finger.

Jacob's Ladder

 Jacob and Esau kept fighting so much that their mother, Rebekkah, was afraid they might each take a זַיִן zayin (weapon) and kill each other.

Rebekkah said,
"Jacob, my precious son,
you must leave here
and find a safe place for a while,
until Esau is not so angry at you anymore."

So Jacob left home
and started walking toward
his Uncle Lavan's house.
When he became tired,
he found some stones
where he could lay down his head.
Soon he fell asleep.

Then Jacob dreamed an amazing dream.

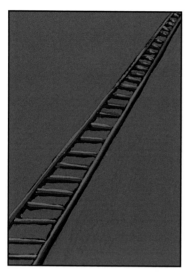

There was a ladder that rose from the earth to the heavens with angels climbing up and down upon it.

God stood over all this and spoke to him.

"I AM THE GOD OF YOUR PARENTS
AND GRANDPARENTS.
THIS LAND YOU ARE LYING UPON RIGHT NOW
IS THE LAND I AM GOING TO GIVE TO YOU
AND YOUR זֶרַע zera (CHILDREN).
YOUR FAMILY WILL SPREAD OUT LIKE SEEDS
IN EVERY DIRECTION,
EAST, WEST, NORTH, AND SOUTH.
THE WHOLE EARTH WILL BE BLESSED
THROUGH YOUR זֶרַע zera(CHILDREN)
AND THROUGH YOUR CHILDREN'S CHILDREN.

"THEY WILL KEEP GROWING LIKE A BEAUTIFUL
GARDEN FULL OF FLOWERS AND FRUITS
AND VEGETABLES OF ALL COLORS AND SHAPES.

"WHEREVER YOU GO, I SHALL ALWAYS BE WITH YOU,
KEEPING YOU SAFE,
KEEPING YOU CLOSE TO THIS LAND YOU LOVE.
IF YOU MUST LEAVE THIS LAND YOU ARE LYING ON,
I SHALL BRING YOU BACK HERE.
I SHALL BE WITH YOU
UNTIL ALL MY PROMISES COME TRUE."

When Jacob awoke, he was afraid.
God had never spoken to him before.
He took the stone
he had rested his head on all night
and stood it up like a pillar.
He poured oil over it.
Then Jacob made a promise,
saying, "If God takes care of me
and my family
as God promised in my dream,
and I can really
go back home in peace,
then I will love God
for the rest of my life,
the way my parents
and grandparents have done.

"I WILL CALL THE PLACE
WHERE THIS STONE NOW STANDS
BET EL, GOD'S HOUSE.
THIS IS WHERE I SAW GOD FOR THE FIRST TIME."

ACTIVITIES

1. *Dance it, move it.* This is a good activity to do in a group. You are an angel, climbing up and down Jacob's Ladder. How would you move? How would you relate to the other angels? What is happening up in the heavens and down on the earth as you go up and down the ladder? Take turns being angels going up and angels going down.

    Someone is Jacob lying down on the ground, having this dream. How would Jacob move as he is dreaming? Does he move at all?

2. Draw a picture of a dream of yours that you remember.

3. Sing "We Are Climbing Jacob's Ladder."

Chapter Eight: HET

חָבֵר
HAVER [FRIEND]

חַיִּים
HAYYIM [LIFE]

Hinting around Het

Have you heard how the letter ה heh caught cold and tried to clear her throat? She tried gargling and sounded just like ח het: Kh-Kh-Kh-Kh. Try it.

ח Het is the strong letter you hear in the word לְחַיִּים L'Hayyim'! To life!

Can you think of a letter in the English alphabet that sounds just like ח het? The sound of "H" and the sound of "K" come closest, but even they do not sound like ח het. ח Het really does not have an English cousin the way so many of the other Hebrew letters do.

Jacob and Rachel

 After Jacob dreamed of the ladder,
he set up a monument
in the place where he had dreamed.
After that, he kept on walking.
At last he reached
his Uncle Lavan's house.

There he met
the beautiful Rachel, Lavan's daughter.
She was bringing her flock of sheep
to the well for a drink.
Right away Jacob kissed her
as he would have kissed
an old חָבֵר haver (friend).
She was, after all, his cousin
whom he had never seen before.

"I am so happy to see you, Rachel.
Your father is my mother's brother,"
explained Jacob.
Rachel was very excited to hear this.
She ran and told her father right away.

Lavan came out to see his sister, Rebekkah's son who had come from so far away.

"How is חַיִּים hayyim (life)
where you come from, my boy?"
Lavan asked Jacob,
hugging and kissing him like a good חָבֵר haver.
"How long can you stay with us?"

Jacob stayed and worked
for his Uncle Lavan.
After one month, Lavan
wanted to pay him.
By this time,
Jacob had become a good
חָבֵר of Rachel's.
Jacob loved Rachel
and wanted to spend his
life with her.

So he said to Lavan,
"I will work for you for seven years
if I can marry Rachel."

Lavan agreed. Jacob worked very hard,
and he loved Rachel so much
that seven years went by like seven days.

Lavan had an older daughter
named Leah,
and nobody was asking for
her hand
in marriage.
Lavan wanted to make sure
that she would be married,
too.
So he made a plan.
At the end of Jacob's seven
years of working,
Lavan made a wedding party.
In those days,
the bride did not come to the party.
She waited until her husband finished
eating and drinking.
Then she would come to him
as he waited for her in the dark, in their bed.

When the party was over,
Lavan brought his daughter
Leah to Jacob.
She was wearing a veil, of course,
and it was so dark that Jacob
could not tell she was not
his beloved Rachel.

In the light of morning,
Jacob saw that he had been tricked.
"Why did you give me Leah
and not Rachel,
for whom I have worked so hard
all these years?"
he demanded angrily of Lavan.

Lavan answered,
"In my land,
the older must be married
before the younger.
Work another seven years for me
and you shall have Rachel, too."

So Jacob worked another seven years
in order to spend the rest of his חַיִּים hayyim
with his Rachel.

ACTIVITIES

1. *Sing songs of* ח het: " Shalom, חֲבֵרִים Haverim" and "לְחַיִּים L'Hayyim!"

   Shalom, חֲבֵרִים Haverim Hello, Friends

   Shalom, חֲבֵרִים Haverim Hello, Friends

   Shalom, Shalom Hello, Hello

   L'Hitraot, L'Hitraot See You Again, See You Again

   Shalom, Shalom Goodbye and Peace.

   *

   To Life, To Life, לְחַיִּים L'Hayyim!

   לְחַיִּים L'Hayyim, לְחַיִּים L'Hayyim, To Life!

2. *To Think About*: Did you ever want something very, very much? Something that was hard for you to get because you just weren't ready yet, or it wasn't there yet? What was it? How did you manage to wait until you could get it?

3. Draw Jacob's face when he discovered that his bride was Leah and not Rachel.

   Draw Leah's face when she realized how disappointed and upset he was.

   Draw Lavan's face when Jacob became angry with him about being tricked.

   Draw Rachel's face when Leah came and told her of the plan.

Chapter Nine: TET

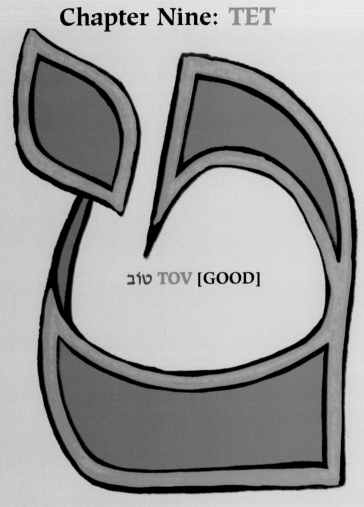

טוב TOV [GOOD]

Talking about ט Tet

Take the letter ט tet. Tickle it till it is terribly tired. Take a tiny, tiny break and tickle it again, this time under the toes. Then make the sound of a train, "TOOT, TOOT!" and try *not* to touch your tongue to your teeth. Is this too much for you? Must be time to talk about the letter ט tet.

As you can tell by now, ט tet sounds like the letter "T." Can you make a ט tet sound *without* touching your tongue to your teeth? Pretty tricky.

Joseph and his Brothers

For many years,
Rachel did not have
any children,
while her sister Leah
kept having
one baby after another.
Rachel was very sad about this.

Then at last Rachel gave birth to a baby boy.
They named the child Joseph.

Jacob loved Joseph best of all,
and the eleven other sons knew it.
Can you guess how they treated
their little brother?
Good טוֹב tov
or bad לֹא טוֹב lo tov?
If you guessed לֹא טוֹב lo tov, you are right!
Joseph's brothers were very jealous of him.
They hardly cared if he lived or died.

Jacob loved Joseph best of all.
He made him a beautiful coat of many colors.
Was this טוֹב tov
or לֹא טוֹב lo tov?
It may have been
טוֹב tov for Joseph,
but it was לֹא טוֹב lo tov
for his brothers.
Joseph loved his coat,
and he wore it everywhere.

Whenever his brothers saw the coat,
they remembered that their father loved Joseph
more than all of them put together.

Joseph had dreams
that he told his brothers and his father.
In his dreams,
Joseph was stronger and bigger
than everyone else.
In his dreams,
the entire family was bowing down to him.

When his brothers heard the dreams,
did they think they were טוֹב
or לֹא טוֹב?
If you guessed לֹא טוֹב, you are right again.

Joseph's brothers were so mad at him
because of his special coat
and his special dreams,
they decided to kill him
and drop him into a big hole full of mud.
That way, they would never have to see him again.

What do you think of this plan?
Was it טוֹב or לֹא טוֹב for Joseph?

Reuben, the oldest brother,
thought this plan was לֹא טוֹב.
He begged his brothers not to kill Joseph
but to throw him into a hole full of mud
and leave him there.
The, Reuben planned to come back later
and rescue Joseph in secret.

He would send him home
when his brothers were not looking.
What sort of a brother was Reuben—
טוב or לֹא טוב?
What would you have done
if you were one of Joseph's brothers?

ACTIVITIES

1. *Joseph's coat*: There were many stories that the Families of Israel used to tell that were not part of the Torah. These stories have been handed down to us, generation after generation, along with the Torah.

   One of these stories is about Joseph's coat of many colors. This coat was so special, there was no other coat like it in the whole world. Not only was it woven of many colors so that it shone like a rainbow, but the material of the coat was as light as a feather, so light that Joseph could crumple the whole coat into the palm of his hand (Ginzberg's *Legends* Vol.II, p.7). Can you imagine such a coat?

   Take a paper bag from the supermarket. Cut it down the middle on one side and through the bottom of the bag. Now the bag needs two holes for arms. Cut these out. Then draw or paint on the bag to make a "coat of many colors." You can also use an old pillowcase and just cut holes in the three seams for your head and arms. Then decorate the "coat" as you like to make it a "coat of many colors."

2. Make a list of טוב tov and לא טוב lo tov for Ways of Behaving; Things That Have Happened This Year; Favorite Stories in Which Things Happen that are טוב tov and לא טוב lo tov.

3. *To think about*: Do you have a brother or a sister? Do you have a cousin, relative, or close friend?

   Do you ever feel that they are 1) more loved or liked than you? 2) getting more attention than you? 3) getting more toys or privileges than you? How do you react? How do your parents, teachers, or the adults nearby handle this? How would you handle it if you were the parent or adult in charge?

Chapter Ten: YUD

יָד YAD (HAND)
יוֹסֵף YOSEF (JOSEPH)
יהוה YUD-HEH-VAV-HEH
(NAME OF GOD)

Yodeling about Yud

Do you know what the smallest letter in the Hebrew alphabet is? You're right if you guessed י yud. It is small, but very important.

י yud stands for the number ten. י yud means יָד yad or "hand" in Hebrew. Put your two hands together, and you have ten fingers. Ten, just like the י yud.

Ten Commandments. Ten Plagues.

Joseph in Egypt

Yes, יוֹסֵף Yosef (Joseph) did make it up out of that big hole. His brothers sold him to a group of traveling merchants who happened to be coming by.

They brought יוֹסֵף Yosef down to Egypt and sold him to a servant of Pharaoh named Potiphar.
Meanwhile, Jacob was sure his son was gone forever. He cried and cried.

Down in Egypt, יוֹסֵף Yosef worked very hard for his master. God was with him as he fixed broken doors, pots, and chairs in the house. He went to the market to buy things.

Whatever the יָד yad (hand) of יוֹסֵף Yosef touched seemed to work better and look better.

Potiphar trusted יוֹסֵף more and more. Finally, Potiphar decided to put יוֹסֵף in charge of the whole house.

Can you imagine?
First יוֹסֵף was thrown into a big hole by brothers who hated him.
Then he became the most trusted worker of an Egyptian chief of Pharaoh!

God stayed very close to יוֹסֵף.
When someone dreamed a strange dream that they could not understand,
they would ask יוֹסֵף to tell them what the dream meant.

Because the יָד yad of God was with him,
יוֹסֵף Yosef easily understood
what the dream meant.

Even Pharaoh heard about the wisdom of יוֹסֵף.
When he had a dream he could not figure out,
he asked יוֹסֵף to tell him what it meant.
יוֹסֵף always knew.

Pharaoh was very happy
to have a man as wise as יוֹסֵף
at the palace.
He took the ring off his יָד yad
and put it on the יָד yad of יוֹסֵף Yosef.
Pharaoh said,
"You shall rule all of Egypt.
Only I shall be above you."

Every time there was a problem
in the land of Egypt,
Pharaoh asked יוֹסֵף what to do.
So יוֹסֵף became very rich and powerful.
Everywhere he went,
people bowed down before him.
Just like in his dreams.

ACTIVITIES

1. *A tzedakah project*: Joseph and his family lived in a time of terrible drought and famine. Joseph made sure that the people of Egypt and his family had enough food and water. He did this by saving supplies while there were plenty for the time when there were hardly any. In your town or city, there are people who do not have enough to eat. Bring some canned goods to a food pantry in your area that distributes food to the hungry.

2. *A comparison tale, The Golden Touch*: There is an expression—Everything he touches turns to gold. This means that whatever the person does turns out well. Even a mistake becomes a wonderful thing. For example, he leaves a bunch of grapes out in the sun, and they turn into raisins, which are even sweeter. This was the way Joseph's life was going. There is another story about someone who had "the golden touch."

    There once was a king of Greece who lived a long time ago. Like Joseph, he had amazing powers in his hands. This came about because he received one wish from the gods. Do you know what he wished? King Midas wished that everything he touched would turn to gold. This was wonderful until he hugged his daughter one day, and *she* became a golden statue.

    Midas begged the gods to turn her back into flesh and blood. In order for this to happen, he would have to lose the golden touch. He happily agreed to this so that his daughter, more precious than gold, would be restored to him.

    Joseph's touch came from God, but it did not *really* turn things into gold. It just made everything turn out well so that Potiphar and Pharoah trusted Joseph and kept rewarding him for all he did. These rewards, in turn, helped Joseph's family survive the famine. Joseph's "golden touch" gave life instead of taking it away, as with King Midas.

Chapter Eleven: KAF

כְּנַעַן KENAA'AN [CANAAN]
כָּל KOL [ALL]

Clues about Kaf

Come and learn about the letter כָּף kaf. What does כָּף kaf look like to you?

Can you make a כָּף kaf shape with your hand? כָּף Kaf is another word for "hand" in Hebrew. יָד Yad means the whole hand with fingers and thumb. כָּף Kaf means the palm of the hand, the inside part that can hold things. כָּף Kaf is a container.

Joseph with His Family Again

כָּל Kol (All)
the containers—
baskets, bags, and pots—
in כְּנַעַן Kena'an (Canaan),
where Joseph's family lived,
were empty.
The land had dried up,
and so Jacob sent his sons to Egypt to buy food.

כָּל Kol the brothers came to Joseph
and bowed down before him to ask for food,
just the way it had happened in his dreams.
Joseph knew who they were at once,
although they did not know their brother at all.

Joseph was very happy to see his brothers,
but he was also sad.
He had been away from home
for such a long time,
he was a stranger in his own family.

He invited his brothers to eat with him,
and they did.
Still they did not know Joseph,
whom they had sold so many years ago.

Then Joseph
could not wait any longer.
He said, "Do you know
that your other brother
is still alive?"
They stared at him in amazement.
"Yes," he said,
"I am Joseph, your brother,
the one you sold down to Egypt
so many years ago.

"Please do not be sad about this
or angry at yourselves
for what you did.
God meant for me
to go down to Egypt
so I could give you food when you needed it.

I am like a father to Pharaoh.
He trusts me so much,
I can get you whatever you need."

The brothers could not believe their eyes.
Here was Joseph, their father's favorite,
who used to wear
the coat of many colors.
Joseph was the one they had thrown
into a big hole and then sold.
Joseph was the one
who ended up in Egypt,
almost as powerful as Pharaoh
for all these years.
They could not say a word.

Then Joseph said,
"Go back to כְּנַעַן and bring my father here.
Tell him I am sending for him,
that I want him to live here,
where there is plenty of food."

So Jacob came to live near Joseph
for the rest of his days.
And Jacob was able to bless
כָּל kol his children before he died.

ACTIVITIES

1. כ Kaf is the first letter of the word כֶּתֶר keter (crown). Make a crown for your head out of paper, cardboard, tin foil, or pipe cleaners. Decorate the crown and make it beautiful.

2. *Dance of כ Kaf*: In some parts of the world, like Thailand and Java, people use their hands the way you might use your feet to dance. Make the palms of your hands into as many shapes as you can. Start with very tight fists and gradually unroll them until your hand is flat as a pancake. Wave your hands around, whirl them and twirl them.

   Make the room dark and shine a flashlight on one wall. Dance with the palms of your hands in front of that wall. See all the different shapes and characters you can make.

3. Pretend you are one of the Mothers or Fathers of the Jewish People. Think of blessings to give to כָּל kol (all) the people you love.

Chapter Twelve: LAMED

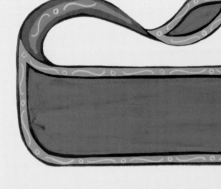

לָמַד
LAMAD [TEACH, LEARN]

לֹא LO [NO, NOT]

לֵוִי LEVI [TRIBE OF LEVI]

Learning with Lamed

ל Lamed is a letter to learn from. It is the twelfth letter of the א–ב alef-bet, standing tall above all the other letters.

ל Lamed makes a sound like the letter "L". La-la-la-la-la-la... sounds like singing.

In Hebrew, the word לָמַד lamad means both "learn" and "teach." Right now, as you read these stories, you are learning Torah the way Jews have been doing for years. Someday you will teach these stories to your friends and family.

Can you guess what one of the most important words in the world is? Go ahead. Take a guess....

Here's a hint: This word is one of the first words a little child learns to say. Do you remember how you used to say "No! No! No!"? ל Lamed begins the Hebrew word for "no."

The Birth of Moses

When the Families of Israel
were in Egypt,
they had to learn to say, "No!"
In Hebrew, the word for "No"
starts with ל lamed.
לֹא Lo! It even sounds like "No!"

The Families of Israel had to say "לֹא Lo"
to Pharaoh, the king of Egypt,
because he had ordered a terrible thing
to be done.

In those days, a baby was born at home
with a midwife
instead of in a hospital
with a doctor.
A midwife is a woman
who helps a woman give birth to her baby.

Pharaoh told the midwives,
"You must not let the baby boys live,
only the baby girls.
You must kill every baby boy
as soon as he is born!"

But the midwives said
to each other secretly,
"לֹא!
We will not do
as Pharaoh says.
We shall let *all*
the babies live."

אֱלֹהִים Elohim was glad
that the midwives
were helping babies
instead of hurting them.
For this
they received a reward.
אֱלֹהִים Elohim gave
them large families
of their own.

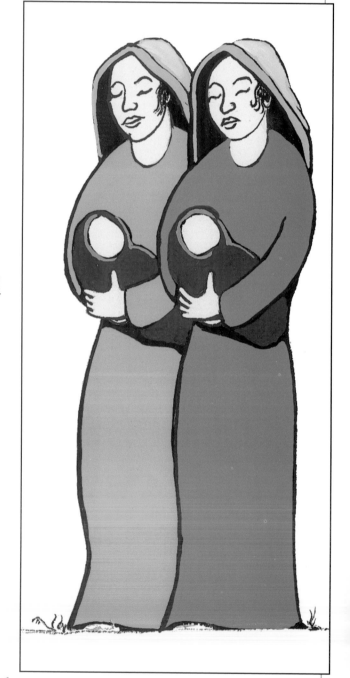

At this time there lived a
husband and wife
named Amram and Yokheved
from the tribe of לֵוִי (Levi).
Yokheved had just given birth
to a new baby boy.
She did not want Pharoah
to find him,
so she said
to her daughter, Miriam,
"Place your baby brother in a little ark
in the middle of the plants
growing by the riverbank."
Miriam did as her mother asked.
Then she stayed to watch
what happened to him.

Meanwhile, Yokheved prayed
that her baby boy would be safe.
She prayed that the wicked Pharaoh
would not find him.
What do you think she said in her prayer?

ACTIVITIES

1. Draw a picture of baby Moses in the ark. Imagine you are this baby. How do you feel? What comforts you?

2. Discuss what you would have done if you were one of the Hebrew midwives and you were supposed to obey Pharoah's evil decree. How would you have handled it?

3. Next to the big ל Lamed, the Learning Letter, make a list of things you would like to learn.

4. Sing a song you know using la-la-la, the sound of ל Lamed. For example, "Row, Row, Row Your Boat," *Hinei Mah Tov,* "This Old Man", *Dona, Dona.*

Chapter Thirteen: MEM

מֹשֶׁה MOSHE [MOSES]
מִצְרַיִם MITZRAYIM [EGYPT]
מִרְיָם MIRIAM [MIRIAM]

Making Mem

Make the sound m-m-m-m-m with your mouth. Maybe you make this sound when you have just eaten your favorite food. Maybe you make this sound when you hum a song to yourself. Mm-mmm-mm-mmm-mm-mmmm….

In the Hebrew alphabet, the letter מ mem makes the "m-m" sound.

Look at the shape of מ mem. Do you see a mouth there? What is amazing about מ mem is that you can write it in two ways, מ or ם, depending on whether it comes at the start or the end of a word. Can you see the difference? The mouth of מ mem can be closed or open, just like your mouth.

Miriam and Moses

מִרְיָם Miriam carried
her baby brother
to the riverbank.
She gently set him down
in the reeds
growing by the banks
of the Nile River.
Then she stepped back
and stood in the shade
of the tallest reeds, where nobody could see her.
מִרְיָם Miriam kept her eyes wide open
to make sure her baby brother was all right.

All this time,
the baby boy had never been alone.
Suddenly, he opened his mouth
and cried loudly.
There was a strange face looking down at him.
The face belonged to the daughter of Pharaoh.
She had been taking a bath in the river
when she noticed the little ark
floating among the reeds.

מִרְיָם Miriam saw
that the princess was ready
to take him
back to the palace.
She said,
"Would you like me
to bring someone
to nurse him for you?"

"Yes. Please." answered Pharaoh's daughter.
"That would be very kind of you."

So מִרְיָם Miriam brought her mother
to care for the baby.

The princess named the
baby מֹשֶׁה Moshe,
"because I drew him out of
the water," she said.
Sometimes in Hebrew a
name tells a story.

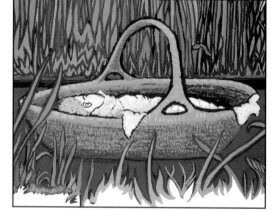

מִצְרַיִם Mitzrayim is the name
the Jewish People gave to Egypt.
מִצְרַיִם Mitzrayim means
"from the narrow places."

For many years,
Egypt was a good place
for the Jewish People to live.
They had plenty of food and clothes.
They worked hard so that they could build
big and beautiful homes for themselves.
Life was good.
The Jews were free and open,
like the first מ mem.

Then things changed.
Pharaoh thought the Jews were too rich,
too many, too happy, and too strong.
He was afraid they would take over מִצְרַיִם
Mitzrayim (Egypt),
so he started to close doors on them,
tight shut like the second ם mem.

If you had a pair of pants
or shoes or a dress that became too small,
then you know the feeling of the Jews
in מִצְרַיִם Mitzrayim, the narrow place.

 מֹשֶׁה Moshe grew up
in the palace of Pharaoh,
raised by his mother
and the princess.
Even though he did not live
with the Hebrews,
he felt very close to them
because he knew that he was one of them.
His mother made sure
מֹשֶׁה Moshe knew who he was,
even though he lived the life of a prince
in Pharaoh's home.

ACTIVITIES

1. Can you think of other names that have stories? How about אָדָם Adam
   (Adam) and אֲדָמָה adamah (earth); יַעֲקֹב Ya'akov (lit. supplanter) (Jacob) and
   יִשְׂרָאֵל Yisrael (lit. one who struggles with God) (Israel); יִצְחָק Yitzhak (lit
   laughter) (Isaac)? What stories do these names tell?

   Do you know the story of your English and Hebrew names? For whom were
   you named? How does your name fit you?

   Do you know any stories of the names of other people in your family?

2. Draw a picture of something narrow and something wide or something open
   and something closed.

3. Make your body narrow and make it wide. How does it feel to be wide and
   narrow? Now make your body closed, and then make it open. Does this feel
   any different?

4. Imagine that you are Pharoah. How do you feel when your daughter brings a
   strange baby boy into your home? What do you do about it?

Chapter Fourteen: NUN

נִין NIN (DESCENDANT, GREAT-GRANDCHILD)

נְבִיאָה NEVI'AH (PROPHETESS)

News about Nun

נ Nun is a letter with two different shapes, one for the beginning of a word נ and one for the end ן, just like the letter מ mem you heard about in the last chapter.

Pretend each of the shapes is a person. What is that person doing?

Now pretend you can move any way you like, as if you were made of clay. Make yourself into each shape of the letter נ nun and see what that shape makes you feel like doing.

נ Nun sounds just like the letter "N" in English. There is a word נִין *nin* in Hebrew that sounds like נ nun. נִין Nin means "great-grandchild." All of us on earth come from the same original parents, the First Man, Adam, and the First Woman, Eve. All the Jews come from Abraham and Sarah. Even Moses was a נִין nin (great-grandchild) of Abraham and Sarah.

Moses and Miriam at the Reed Sea

When Moses was old enough,
he left Pharaoh's palace.
He came to live
in the wilderness,
where he worked
as a shepherd.
He got married
and had a son.

One day while Moses was tending his sheep,
God decided to test him.
God wanted to see if Moses was ready
to have a talk.
The test God used was a נֵס nes (miracle).

As Moses was walking,
he saw something that seemed hard to believe.
He saw a bush burning and burning,
yet it did not burn down at all.
How could this נֵס nes be happening?

Moses was trying to figure this out
when suddenly God spoke to him
from inside the burning bush.

"MOSES," said God,
"I AM THE GOD OF YOUR FATHER
AND MOTHER,
THE GOD OF ABRAHAM AND SARAH,
THE GOD OF ISAAC AND REBEKKAH,
THE GOD OF JACOB, RACHEL, AND LEAH.
I HAVE SEEN HOW EACH
נִין nin (GREAT-GRANDCHILD)
OF THEIRS HAS BECOME A SLAVE.
I HAVE SEEN THEM SUFFER.
I WANT YOU TO TAKE THEM OUT OF EGYPT
TO THE LAND OF MILK AND HONEY."

When God spoke,
Moses was very humble,
just like the letter נ nun.
He bent his head
and put his hands up
in front of his face
because he was afraid
to look at God.

At first,
Moses did not feel strong enough
or brave enough
to do what God had told him to do.
Still, he came to Pharaoh and said,
"Let my people go!"
But Pharoah said, "NO!"

Pharaoh was so stubborn
that Moses had to teach him a lesson.
With the help of God and his brother,
Moses brought Ten Plagues upon Egypt.

Even after the Ten Plagues,
Pharaoh would not let the slaves leave Egypt.
But one night the slaves escaped.

By this time, Moses was stronger
and much more sure of himself.
Like the beginning ‫נ‬ nun,
he could bend his head the way a servant does.
Like the ending ‫ן‬ nun,
he could stand tall and proud.

The Egyptian army rode
after the Families of Israel

to bring them back to Egypt
to be slaves again.
But Moses stretched out his hand,
and a נֵס nes happened.
The waters of the sea opened,
and the Families of Israel
walked though onto the dry land!

Miriam,
Moses' sister,
led the women
in songs and dances
while Moses led the men.
Miriam was a prophetess,
someone God calls on
to speak to the people.

In Hebrew, the word
for "prophet," נָבִיא navi,
starts with the letter נ nun,
the נ nun
that bends its head
to hear what God is saying.

Miriam was a נְבִיאָה nevi'ah
(prophetess)
who sang the words
she heard from God.
Moses was a teacher
who taught the words.
Together, Miriam and Moses
made sure that
the Families of Israel understood
what God wanted them to do.
Together they taught
the Families of Israel
how to change
from being bent-over slaves
like the beginning נ
to proud people standing free and tall
like the final ן.

ACTIVITIES

1. *To look up:* Look in a Haggadah together to see what the Ten Plagues were. Also, for an excellent portrayal of the plagues for young readers, see *The Ten Plagues of Egypt* by Shoshana Lepone (New York: The Judaica Press, 1988).

2. *To Discuss*: Who are some prophets and prophetesses today? Name them and explain how they are prophets.

3. *You are there at the crossing of the Sea of Reeds:* Block out a space in the room to be the "sea." Use a blanket or old sheet or tablecloth for the "water." Have two people on either side of the blanket make "waves" by moving the cloth. Select a "Moses" and the rest should take the parts of the Families of Israel.

   Pretend you are there as the Sea of Reeds parts. How do you feel? How would you walk across the dry land? What is in your mind as you are crossing to the other side? What is in your mind when you see the army of Pharoah drowning behind you?

Chapter Fifteen: SAMEKH

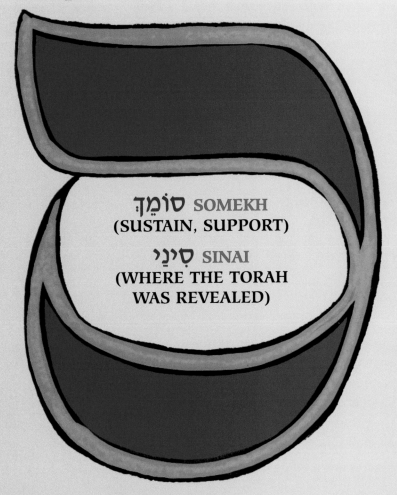

סוֹמֵךְ SOMEKH
(SUSTAIN, SUPPORT)

סִינַי SINAI
(WHERE THE TORAH
WAS REVEALED)

Samekh Says

"You can count on me," the letter ס samekh says. See how
ס samekh sits, all sealed up tight.

ס Samekh is a letter that surrounds space. Put your two thumbs
together, and then put your two pointer fingers together to form a
circle. You have made a ס samekh. Now take your ס samekh and
make a frame around something you want to look at more closely.
What do you see?

At Mount Sinai

For three months
after they left Egypt
and crossed the Reed Sea,
the Families of Israel
wandered in the wilderness.
Finally they reached
Mount סִינַי Sinai,
and there they camped.

This was the mountain
where Moses had seen the burning bush.

At סִינַי Sinai
the Families of Israel
became the Jewish People.
They understood
that they had to stop acting like slaves
without minds of their own
and behave like free people instead.

What does it mean to be free?
You have choices.
The Jewish People chose to listen to Moses.

Moses told them everything God taught him,
all the rules they were supposed to follow
in order to live a good life.
Ten of these rules,
the most important ones of all,
are called the Ten Commandments.

The Ten Commandments
are a safe circle surrounding
the Jewish People.
This is like the letter ס
samekh,
which is a circle surrounding
the space in the middle.
In Hebrew, the word for "help"
or "support"
is סוֹמֵךְ somekh.

God gave the Ten Commandments
to Moses as a gift
to support the Jewish People forever.

These are the Ten Commandments:

1. I am **Adonai,** your God, who took you out of Egypt, who freed you from slavery.

2. You will have no other gods but Me.

3. You will not say my name in vain.

4. Remember the Sabbath day, the day of rest, and do not do any work on that day.

5. Honor your mother and your father.

6. Do not kill.

7. Do not try to take somebody else's husband or wife.

8. Do not steal.

9. Do not lie.

10. Do not try to get what belongs to somebody else.

ACTIVITIES

1. Try to find an example for each commandment. Which of the Ten Commandments do you think is the hardest to obey? Which is the easiest?

2. Every Jew was supposed to be there at Mount Sinai. Even though you had not been born yet, you were there. Draw a picture of yourself at Mount Sinai.

3. Dance the way a slave might dance, and then dance as a free person would dance. What are the differences?

Chapter Sixteen: AYIN

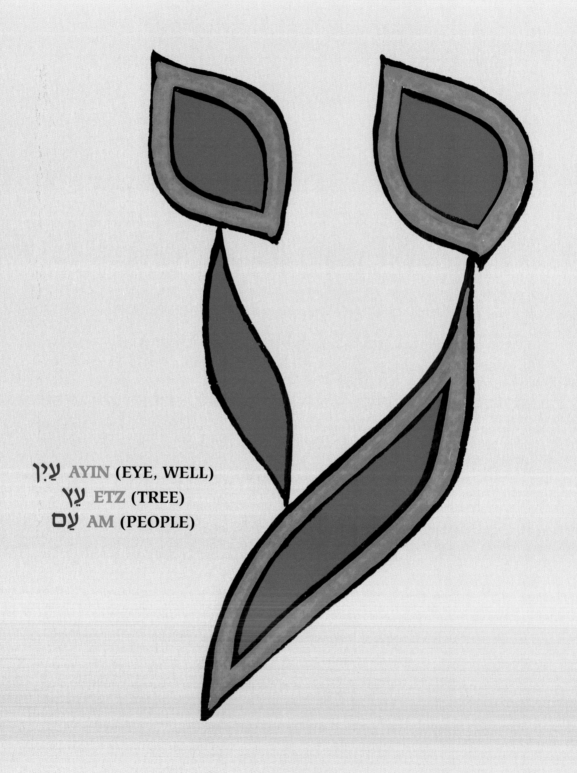

עַיִן AYIN (EYE, WELL)
עֵץ ETZ (TREE)
עַם AM (PEOPLE)

Echoes of Ayin

If you want to find out about a letter that is like a chameleon, then take a look at ע ayin. A chameleon is an animal that changes color whenever it is in a different place. On a green leaf, it's green. On a brown branch, it's brown.

ע Ayin is like that, too. When ע ayin starts the word עֵץ etz (tree), it sounds like "eh". When it starts the word עַם am (people), it sounds like "ah".

When is an eye like a well?

The letter ע ayin is also a word that means "eye". The ע ayin says, "Look at the world. What do you see?"

Do this right now. What do you see in this room? Name five things. How do you know what these things are? Your eyes see and then tell you what they see. Your eyes are like two buckets going down, down, down into a well to find words for what you are seeing.

Some people call the Torah a well—מַעְיָן הַתּוֹרָה ma'yan ha-Torah (Well of Torah). The Torah is a well of living words, of living waters. Learning a word in the Torah is like taking a drink of water at a cool oasis in the desert.

Building the Holy Temple

When Moses gave the Torah
to עַם יִשְׂרָאֵל Am Yisrael
(the People of Israel),
he was giving them words
to keep them alive.
Words like water.

God said to Moses,
"Let the עַם יִשְׂרָאֵל Am Yisrael
make Me a special tent so I can live
among them.
Make it a place where the Torah can be kept."

God told Moses how to make this tent
that could be carried through the desert
as the עַם Am traveled to the Promised Land.
The ark, which held the Torah,
was made of עֵץ etz (wood) and gold.

The special place where the ark was kept
had curtains of goats' hair
and curtains of fine cloth
dyed blue, purple, and red.
The tent around the ark was covered
with animal skins.
On the inside,
the tent was held up by wooden boards
covered with gold.

All the עַם Am gave
whatever they had brought with them
from Egypt
to make this beautiful tent
where God and the Torah could live.

When the tent was all finished,
a wonderful thing happened:
A cloud covered the tent,
and it was filled with God's glory.
As long as the cloud
stayed on top of the tent,
עַם יִשְׂרָאֵל Am Yisrael
stayed where they were.
When the cloud lifted
up and off the tent,
they began walking
to the Promised Land.
This was how they knew
when to travel and when to rest.

עַם יִשְׂרָאֵל kept going
until they reached the Promised Land.

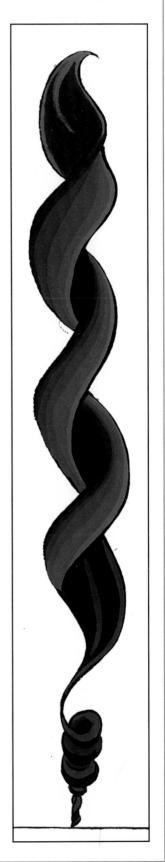

ACTIVITIES

1. In those days of long ago, the sanctuary must have been quite a sight to see. Can you see it in the **ayin** (eye) of your imagination? Pretend you are traveling with the Jewish People. What would you bring to help build the special tent? Make a model or draw a picture of it.

2. Look through a book on Jewish synagogues through the ages. See *Building Jewish Life: Synagogue Activity Book* (Los Angeles: Torah Aura Productions, 1990). Where are the ark and the eternal light in your synagogue or temple?

Chapter Seventeen: PEH

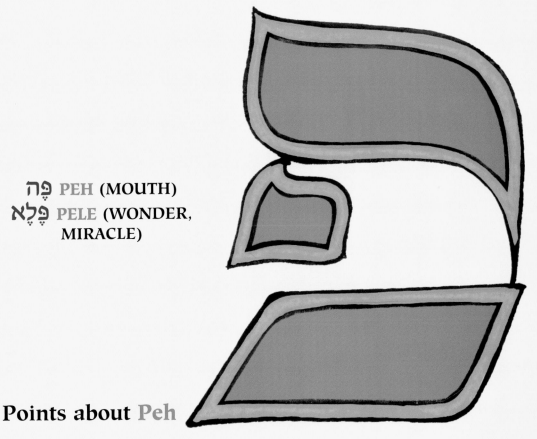

פֶּה PEH (MOUTH)
פֶּלֶא PELE (WONDER,
MIRACLE)

Points about Peh

Please pay attention to the letter פ peh. Pick a letter from the English alphabet that sounds like פ peh…. That's right—"P."

Please pay attention to how you make the "P" sound. What do your lips need to do to make a "P?"

First, you close your lips all the way without making a sound. Then suddenly you make a big puff of air through your closed lips, and they pop open. Try it.

Perhaps you have noticed something pretty puzzling about פ peh and "P." First your mouth is shut tight, and then it is open wide.

In Hebrew, the word פֶּה peh means "mouth." Can you find the mouth of the letter פ peh?

The Prayers of Hannah

A long, long time
after the Families of Israel
reached the Promised Land,
there lived a family
in the hills north of Jerusalem.
There was a man
named Elkanah,
and he had two wives,
Hannah and Penina.

This man's life was perfect
except for one thing.
While Penina kept having
one baby after another,
Hannah had no children at all.

Hannah was very sad about this.
She wanted to be a mother.
She wanted children.
She wanted to help them grow,
answer their questions,
and ask them some of her own.
Every day she prayed to God to
give her a child,
but still nothing happened.

Hannah became so sad,
she didn't feel like eating or sleeping.
All she could do
was open her פֶּה peh (mouth)
and cry and cry.

Elkanah did not know what to do.
He loved Hannah and wanted her to be happy.
He said, "Hannah, what does it matter
if you don't have children?
Aren't I better than ten sons?
Please stop crying and feeling so sad."

But Hannah could not stop.

One day, the whole family—
Elkanah, Hannah, Penina,
and all the children—
went to pray and give thanks to God
at the Tabernacle near Jerusalem.
When they were ready to leave,
Hannah said, "I want to stay a little longer.
I haven't finished praying yet."
So the family left her to pray by herself.

Once she felt that she was alone with God,
she began to pour her heart out.
She opened her פֶה peh
and talked about everything
that was on her mind.
She cried enough tears
for an ocean with ships sailing on it.
She began to feel a little better.

Now Eli, the priest,
was watching
Hannah pray,
and he saw something
very strange.
Hannah's פֶּה peh
was open,
and her lips were moving,
but no sound came out.

"She must not really be praying,"
he said to himself.
"She must have drunk too much wine."

Suddenly, he started yelling at Hannah
at the top of his lungs.
"You should be ashamed.
Get out of this holy place.
There is no room here for drinking
and acting silly."

Hannah looked at him with sad eyes.
"I have not been drinking, sir;
I have only been pouring out my heart to God.
You see, I want a child so much,
and I have none."

Eli was ashamed of his mistake.
He told Hannah,
"Go in peace, and God will make
a פֶּלֶא pele (Miracle).
God will grant you your wish."

For the first time in many years,
Hannah was happy.
She returned to Elkanah
with hope in her heart.
Not too long after this,
a פֶּלֶא pele did happen.
Hannah gave birth to Samuel,
who became a prophet,
a wise and good man
who helped people his whole life.

ACTIVITIES

1. Hannah is the model of Jewish prayer. She teaches us the way we are supposed to pray. In silence. From the heart. Think about a miracle that you would like to happen. Make up a prayer for that miracle. Say it silently to yourself, and then have somebody help you write it down.

2. Pretend you are in the Temple with Hannah and Eli. Have someone take each part. How does it feel to be Hannah? Eli? Could you do something different from what Eli did? What would it be?

Chapter Eighteen: TZADI

צֶדֶקֶת TZADEKET
(KIND, GIVING WOMAN)

צְבָתִים TZVATIM
(BUNDLES OF GRAIN)

צְדָקָה TZEDAKAH
(RIGHTEOUS GIVING)

Sounds of Tzadi

Did you know that a letter could grow? Look at tzadi, the eighteenth letter of the Hebrew alphabet. As it pushes up through the dry red earth, צ tzadi reaches for air and sun and rain. Listen to the sound of צ tzadi. Tz-tz-tz-tz-tz... What does that sound like? A cricket chirping? A plant growing? Rain dropping on the dry red earth? What do you hear?

Tz-tz-tz-tz-tz...

The Story of Ruth

Because the Land of Israel
is such a dry place,
a drop of water
is more precious than gold.
Plants and trees can grow only
when there is enough water
for their roots and leaves
to drink.
Today, if there is not enough rain,
we drink a little less water.
We stop watering our lawns
and washing our cars so much.
But we still have enough to eat.

Long ago in the Land of Israel,
when the rains did not come at the right time,
all living things dried up,
and there was a famine.
A famine is when there is not enough food
for all the people living on the land.

Long ago in the Land of Israel,
everyone went hungry and
some people even died during a famine.

Once, at a hard time like this,
there lived two women named Ruth and Naomi.
Ruth had been married to Naomi's son.
That made Naomi her mother-in-law.

Ruth and Naomi
were both very sad because
their husbands had just died.
They had no one in the world
except each other.
They decided to go back to
Naomi's birthplace,
a town called Bethlehem.
There they would start new
lives for themselves.

When they arrived,
Naomi's old friends
gathered around them, saying,
"Naomi is back! Naomi is back!"
They were very happy to see her,

and they wanted to know who Ruth was
and why they were in Bethlehem.

 "Ruth is my daughter-in-law,"
said Naomi.
"She was married to my
beloved son.
First my husband died
and then my son,
Ruth's husband, died.
I told Ruth,

'Go back to your mother's house now.
There is no reason for you to stay
with an old woman like me.
Go. After a time, you will find a new husband,
and you will have many beautiful children.'

"But," continued Naomi,
"Ruth would not go back home.
She said, 'Naomi, I am part of *your* family now.
Your people is my people,
and your God is my God.
You have been so kind to me.
I will never leave you.'

"So you see, my daughter-in-law is
a צַדֶּקֶת tzadeket (a good woman).
She thinks of what is right for others
before she thinks of what is right for herself.

She is very wise
because she knows
that the good deeds
she does are like seeds.
She has planted
many such seeds.
She has watered them well
and given them plenty of sun.
One day she will gather
the fruits of her labors into many
צְבָתִים tz'vatim (bundles).
Then she and I will rejoice at this great harvest."

That night, as Naomi and Ruth were going to bed,
Ruth said, "Tomorrow
I shall follow the people who are picking corn.
Whatever they drop, I shall pick up,
and we shall have something to eat."

That was the custom in Israel.
Poor people would gather צְבָתִים tz'vatim
from whatever the crop-pickers dropped
on the ground.
In this way, the rich people
who owned the fields were able
to help the poor people who had nothing to eat.
When one person gives this kind of help,
that is called צְדָקָה tzedakah (righteous giving).
In those days,
it was very hard for a woman
without a husband or children
to get enough food.
But she could pick up
what was left in the fields
and eat that.
צְדָקָה tzedakah helped her live.

The next day, Ruth went out to work in the fields.
The field where she was working
belonged to a cousin of Naomi's.
His name was Boaz.

As he walked by to check on his workers,
he noticed a beautiful young woman
whom he had never seen before.

"Who is she?" Boaz asked one of the workers.

"Her name is Ruth,
and she has come with Naomi,"
the worker replied.
"Both their husbands have died,
and now each woman
takes care of the other."

Every day
Boaz came out to see his fields
and stopped to talk to Ruth.
He saw how hard she worked,
picking up the corn
that had been dropped
on the ground.
He knew that she did not
think about what she would get.
She thought only about
helping Naomi,
who was too old to go out into the fields herself.

Ruth was, indeed, a **צַדֶּקֶת** tzadeket.
Ruth saw how much Boaz cared for his workers,
as well as for her and Naomi.

One day, Boaz asked Ruth to marry him
and she said, "Yes, I will marry you."
So Boaz and Ruth were married
and they had a son named Oved.
Naomi loved that child
as if he were her own grandson,
so grateful was she for the way Ruth
had cared for her
after her husband and son had died.

Ruth and Boaz raised Oved
to know all about the ways of **צְדָקָה** tzedakah
and helping others.
They taught him that the good deeds you do
are seeds that grow into wonderful fruits
you will harvest the rest of your life.
And Oved, the son of Ruth and Boaz,
became the grandfather of David,
the wise and kind king of Israel.

ACTIVITIES

1. The tradition of צְדָקָה tzedakah (righteous giving) is a very important part of being a Jew. Find places in your town where you can give food or clothing to people who need it. Organize a group to collect food and clothes, and then deliver them.

2. *Movement/dance:* The Ethiopian Jews have a holiday called <u>Sigd</u> where they climb a mountain and re-enact the Giving of the Torah at Mount Sinai. Other Jews celebrate *Shavuot,* which commemorates the same event and is in the spring. We also read the Book of Ruth at that time.

   Do a dance of walking up a steep mountain to receive the Torah. Have people take turns being Moses, who first receives the Torah from God and then gives it to the Jewish People.

3. Ruth and Naomi are two good friends. Do you have a good friend?

   Ruth is a צַדֶּקֶת tzadeket (a wise and good woman). Do you know a צַדֶּקֶת tzadeket or a tzadik? Ask your parents, grandparents, teachers, or friends if they know a good and wise person like Ruth.

Chapter Nineteen: KUF

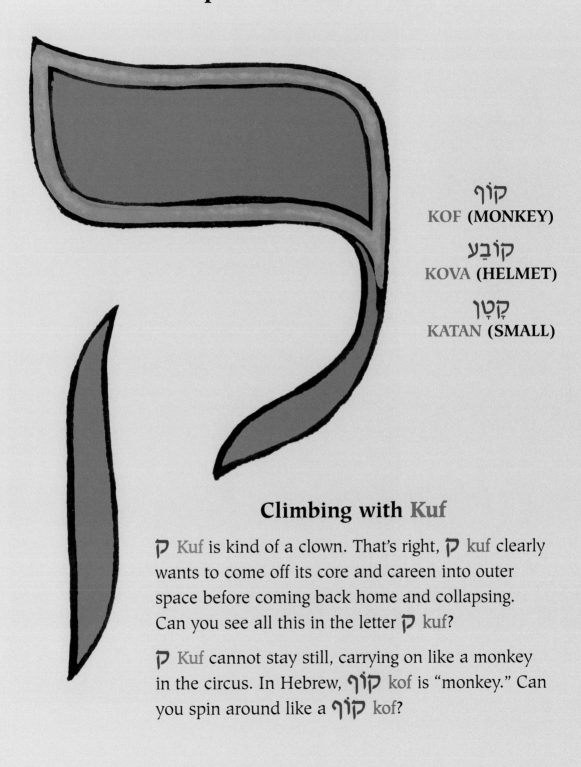

קוֹף
KOF (MONKEY)

קוֹבַע
KOVA (HELMET)

קָטָן
KATAN (SMALL)

Climbing with Kuf

ק Kuf is kind of a clown. That's right, ק kuf clearly wants to come off its core and careen into outer space before coming back home and collapsing. Can you see all this in the letter ק kuf?

ק Kuf cannot stay still, carrying on like a monkey in the circus. In Hebrew, קוֹף kof is "monkey." Can you spin around like a קוֹף kof?

David and Goliath

When David,
the great-grandson of Ruth,
was growing up,
the Families of Israel
had many enemies
who wanted to take over
the Land of Israel.

The Philistines were one enemy.
Goliath was a Philistine who was nine feet tall.

When Goliath saw that the men of Israel
were going to fight the Philistines,
he said, "No, no, no.
Do not send all these men to fight us.
I will fight one of you.
Whoever wins shall rule the other forever.
Now, who will it be?"

David was the קָטָן katan (small one)
of his family, the youngest of eight sons.
He heard of this terrible giant Goliath.
He was not afraid, even though all his brothers
were. Sometimes, the smallest is the bravest.

David said,
"I will fight this terrible giant,
and I will kill him!"

Goliath was dressed
in a full suit of armor
with brass covering his whole body,
arms, legs, and chest.
He wore a brass
קוֹבַע kova (helmet) on his head.
He carried
a thick and sharp wooden spear.

Saul, the king of Israel, gave David
his own suit of armor, but it was too heavy.
He chose to go out and fight Goliath
with only a big stick,
a bag with five smooth stones in it,
and his slingshot.

When Goliath saw David,
the קָטָן katan, he was angry,
"What? Do you think you're going to hurt me
with those sticks and stones?
Come here,
I'm going to serve you
to the birds and beasts
for dinner!"

David answered,
"You think you
are so strong and
powerful,
but God is stronger
and even more powerful
than you!
God does not like people who start battles
for no reason,
so I am going to have to teach you a lesson."
He took a stone from his bag
and shot it right at Goliath with his slingshot.
Goliath fell over dead,
and the Families of Israel
did not have to be afraid of him anymore.

David became one of the greatest kings of Israel.
He was a strong man,
a good thinker,
and a singer of beautiful songs.

ACTIVITIES

1. **Songs of circles and hats**: King David used to sing tunes he made up as he played on his harp. Here are some songs you can sing about the letter ק kuf. ק kuf comes from the word that means "going around and around." Like the seasons of the year, like the earth in space, like the round Torah scroll whose stories we read over and over again each year. Can you think of other things that go around and around? *The Wheels on the Bus Go Round and Round. The Circle Game*—Joni Mitchell. *We Circle Around*—Native American. *My Hat, It Has Three Corners* (*ha-kova sheli shalosh pinot*).

2. Make a pinwheel in the shape of the letter ק kuf. The straight line of the ק kuf is the pinwheel's stick. Attach the curvy "head" of the ק kuf to the stick so it can freely spin.

3. Can you think of a way besides fighting that David could have taught Goliath a lesson?

Chapter Twenty: RESH

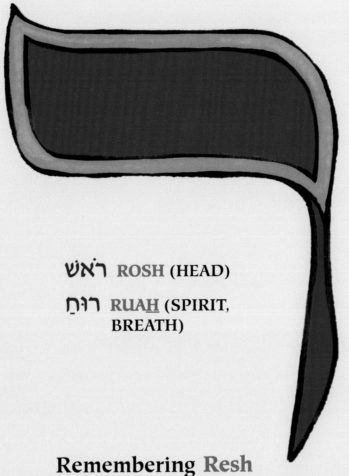

רֹאשׁ **ROSH** (HEAD)

רוּחַ **RUAH** (SPIRIT, BREATH)

Remembering Resh

Race over here right away! ר Resh is a letter that really knows what to do—run in a relay race, ride on a roller coaster, or just relax. You see, ר resh knows what to do because it has a רֹאשׁ rosh (head) on its shoulders.

In Hebrew, ר resh sounds like רֹאשׁ rosh which means "head" or "beginning." רֹאשׁ הַשָּׁנָה Rosh ha-Shanah is the head or beginning of the year. Where is your רֹאשׁ rosh (head)? Now, use your head to figure out which English letter sounds like ר resh. You are right if you said "R."

The Wise
King Solomon

Solomon was the son of King David
and his wife, Bath-Sheva.
He became king of Israel
while he was still a boy
and his father, David, was still alive.

Solomon wanted to be a good king.
He wanted to be fair to his people.
He wanted them to be happy
and to live their lives by the Torah.
He wanted Israel to be a peaceful place
where nobody ever was hungry or homeless.
Solomon means "peace."

One night God came to Solomon in a dream
and said, "What would you like me to give
you?"

Solomon answered,
"I am so young,
and I don't know very much.
I do know that you loved
my father, David.
You helped him rule Israel
wisely and well.
Please give me
a רֹאשׁ rosh (head)
full of wisdom

and a רוּחַ rua<u>h</u> (spirit) full of understanding.
Then I shall be able to rule my people
as they deserve to be ruled."

God was very pleased
with what Solomon had asked for.
God said,
"You have not asked for gold and silver.
You have not asked for a long life for yourself.
You have not asked
to win against all your enemies.
Now I shall grant you the wisdom
and understanding you asked for.

"Because you do not think only of yourself,
I shall give you riches and honor, too.
You will be the greatest king
who has ever lived."

Solomon did become a great king of Israel.
Whenever someone had a question
that nobody else could figure out,
they would come to King Solomon.
He always had an answer, because
God gave him enough wisdom
and understanding to reach the heavens.
God also gave him a heart so big
it stretched as far as the sands
upon the shore of the sea.

ACTIVITIES

1. *Riddle time*: King Solomon was famous for being able to figure out the riddles he was asked by a certain queen, the Queen of Sheba. What riddles do you know? Can you make up one or two new riddles to try out on your friends?

2. *To think about*: If you could ask for anything in the world the way King Solomon did, what would you ask for?

3. Draw a big letter ר resh and a big letter R. Use your imagination and decorate them.

Chapter Twenty-one: SHIN

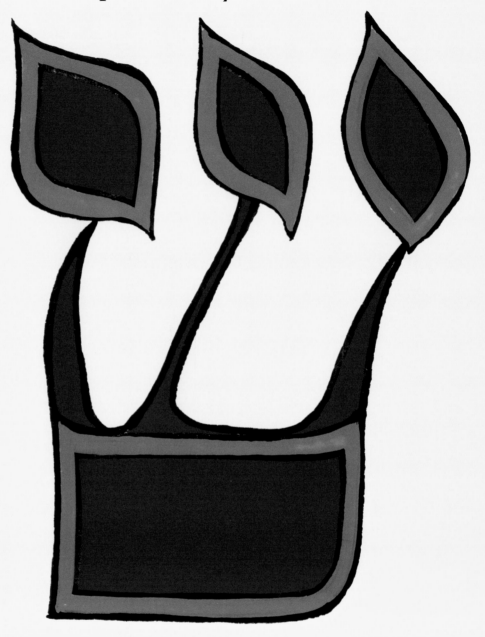

שֵׁן SHEN (TOOTH)
שָׁלוֹם SHALOM (PEACE, HELLO, GOOD-BYE)
שׁוּשָׁן SHUSHAN (CAPITAL OF ANCIENT PERSIA,
WHICH IS IRAN TODAY)

Shouting about Shin

Show me a letter with a tooth שֵׁן shen in three place,s and I'll show you the letter שׁ shin. Can you find a tooth שֵׁן shen in this letter?

If you open your mouth, click your top שֵׁן shen (tooth) to your bottom שֵׁן shen (tooth), and try to push air through, you will make the sound of שׁ shin. Sh-sh-sh-sh-sh-sh-sh-sh-sh...

Sh-sh-sh-sh-sh-sh-sh is the sound you make when a baby is shrieking and you're holding her, trying to calm her down.

Sh-sh-sh-sh-sh-sh-sh-ooooooooooooooh is the sound the waves make as they ride toward shore.

Whoo-oo-oo-sh-sh-sh is the sound the wind makes in the shivering pine trees at night.

Sh-sh-sh-sh-sh-sh-sh is a peaceful sound, a quiet sound. In Hebrew, the word for peace is שָׁלוֹם shalom. Sh-sh-sh-ah-ah-ah-ah-lo-o-o-o-m-m-m-m... Feel the peace inside.

How Queen Esther Saved the Jews

There were many times
when the Jewish People
did not feel peaceful or safe.
There were other times
when peace and freedom lasted.
In Egypt,
when the Jews were slaves,
life was terrible.
Under King Solomon many years later,
peace and freedom ruled again.

Centuries after King Solomon,
in a place called שׁוּשָׁן Shushan,
the capital of the Persian empire,
a city called Qal'a-e-Shush in Iran today,
not far from Israel,
there lived a foolish king named Ahashuerus.
He was not Jewish,
but there were many Jews living in his kingdom.

One day, King Ahashuerus ordered his wife, Queen Vashti, to come before all his friends and show off her beauty. Without any clothes on!

The queen said, "No!" She did not care if there was שָׁלוֹם shalom (peace) in their home or not. She did not wish to parade without any clothes before her husband and his friends.

So King Ahashuerus threw Queen Vashti out of the kingdom. Still, his problems were not over. Now he needed a new wife. He decided to have the most beautiful young women in the kingdom come before him. He would choose the loveliest of them all to be the new queen.

At this time
there lived in the kingdom of Ahashuerus
a young Jewish woman named Esther.
She lived with her uncle, Mordecai.
When Mordecai heard
the king was looking for a wife,
he knew that his niece, Esther would be perfect.
She was very beautiful and very good.

Mordecai brought Esther
to the palace.
As soon as King Ahashuerus
set eyes on her,
he knew she was the one.
So Esther became
Queen of שׁוּשָׁן Shushan.

This would have been a time of שָׁלוֹם
and happiness in the kingdom, but for one man.
He was one of the king's closest friends.
His name was Haman.

Haman hated anyone
who would not bow down before him.
Mordecai did not bow down
to any person on earth,
for a Jew only bows before God.
This made Haman angry, because he liked to
pretend that he was as powerful as the king.

Since Mordecai was a Jew,
Haman decided to kill all the Jews
in שׁוּשָׁן Shushan.
He told his idea to the king.

"Your Royal Highness,"
explained Haman to Ahashuerus,
"there is a people living in שׁוּשָׁן
who are different from the rest of us.
Instead of obeying your laws,
Your Majesty, they obey their own.
We must get rid of them."

"As you say, Haman," agreed the foolish king.
"Do whatever you wish, with my blessing."

Haman sent out a letter to everyone in the land.
The letter said that every Jew—
man, woman, and child—
should be killed.
You can imagine how Queen Esther felt
when her Uncle Mordecai told her
about Haman's terrible plan.

Esther had to think
of something
to stop Haman.
She invited
her husband,
Ahashuerus,
and Haman
to a special feast.
There were all kinds
of tasty foods to eat
and wines to drink.
The king and Haman
enjoyed the feast
very much.

Then the king asked,
"My dear Esther, what is it you wish from me?
You only have to say the word,
and I will do whatever you like,
even give you half my kingdom."

Queen Esther replied,
"If you truly love me,
Oh great and powerful king,
then take away the terrible command
to kill me and my people."

King Ahashuerus was very surprised by this.
He said, "But who has commanded this?"

Esther answered,
"It is your servant you trust so much,
the wicked Haman, who has done this."

"Then hang him at once!"
commanded the king
as Haman froze in fear.

So Haman was put to death
while Esther and Mordecaiand all the rest of the
Jews went free.

That is why we read the Scroll of Esther
with great joy on Purim.
We sing and dance.
We eat and drink
and dress up in costumes.
We remember how Queen Esther saved the Jews
and brought שָׁלוֹם to שׁוּשָׁן once again.

ACTIVITIES

1. Sing songs of peace
   a. *Heveinu Shalom Aleychem*
      (We bring peace to you)
   b. *Oseh Shalom B'mromav* (God
      makes peace in the heavens)
      Hu Ya'aseh Shalom Aleynu
      (God will continue to make
      peace for us) *V'al Kol Yisrael*
      (And for all of Israel) *V'imru
      Amen* (And we'll say "Amen")
   c. We Ain't Gonna Study War No
      More
   d. Blowin' in the Wind
2. *To discuss* : Do you know of any
   countries today or in recent
   history that have made official
   decrees against the Jews? Against
   other people?
3. *Purimshpiel:* With simple
   costumes or with only hats for
   dressing up, act out the Purim
   story.

Chapter Twenty-two: TAV

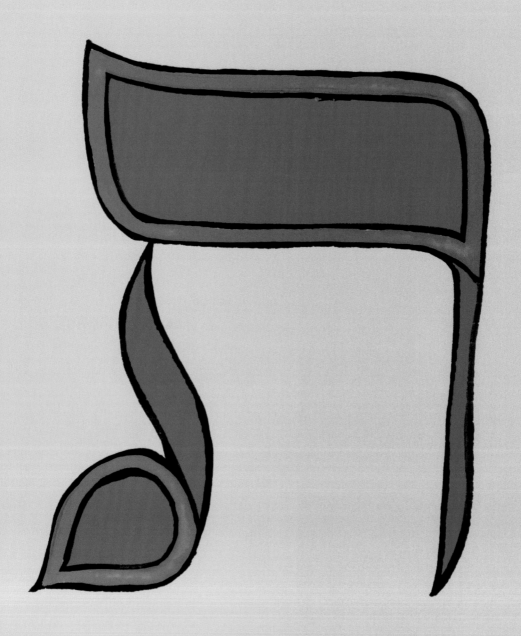

תּוֹרָה TORAH (FIVE BOOKS OF MOSES)
תְּפִלָּה T'FILLAH (PRAYER)

Talking about Tav

At the very end of the Hebrew alphabet, the letter ת tav stands firm and tall. The word ת tav in Hebrew means a mark or a sign.

There are places in the Land of Israel where the desert stretches for miles and miles and nothing grows at all. Then, suddenly, in the middle of that emptiness are some signs of life: a palm tree with dates hanging from its branches like jewels from a necklace; a cactus with sweet fruits waiting to be picked; a blue-robed shepherd girl guiding her flock of sheep along a river bed for a grassy meal. ת Tav is like one of those signs of life in the middle of the desert.

Think of a תּוֹרָה Torah scroll before the scribe has written on it. Parchment the color of sand stretches out like a desert where nothing grows. Then the scribe begins to write, and there is a letter, then a word, a sentence, a whole story. These are the signs that this תּוֹרָה Torah is coming to life. The word תּוֹרָה Torah starts with the letter ת tav.

Daniel

The story of Daniel
comes near the end of the Bible.
It comes after the stories of
Adam and Eve,
Abraham and Sarah,
Jacob, Rachel and Leah,
Joseph, Moses, Miriam, Hannah, Ruth,
David, Solomon, and Esther.
It comes after all the stories
you have read so far in this book.

Daniel was a young boy in ancient Israel
who was handsome and wise.
He thought hard about many different things.
What would he be when he grew up?
Would God always be there to help him?
Why was it that God seemed to talk
to certain people and not to others?

One day King Nebuchadnezzar,
a stranger to Israel,
came to Jerusalem
with his soldiers.
He conquered the holy city.
He told his servants to find
the handsomest and smartest
Jewish boys
in the land to live in his palace.
The king wanted these boys
to help him rule his kingdom
when they became a little older.
King Nebuchadnezzar knew
that the Jews were very wise and just.
Daniel was chosen to live in the palace.

It may sound funny to you,
but in those days,
a king often ruled by whatever
he had dreamed the night before.
Whenever King Nebuchadnezzar had a dream
that he could not understand,
he called upon his wise men
to tell him its meaning.

When they could not figure out
the meaning of the dream,
the king called on Daniel
to tell him what he thought.

Daniel said a תְּפִלָּה t'fillah (prayer) to God,
and he was able to understand
the meaning of the dream.
A תְּפִלָּה t'fillah is a way of speaking to God.
Some people like to speak to God
in a house of prayer with other people.
Others like to speak to God
alone wherever they happen to be,
in their house or outdoors.
Some people like to ask God questions,
and some like to tell God how they are feeling—
thankful or happy or sad.

Daniel used to speak to God in תְּפִלָּה everyday.
He would ask God
what the king's dream meant.
As soon as he received an answer,
he told the king.

The king was so happy,
he thanked Daniel with all his heart.
He gave Daniel many presents
and let him help rule the kingdom as well.

Daniel helped King Nebuchadnezzar
for many years.
After this king died,
other kings came to the throne.
Daniel helped them, too.
He told them the meanings of their dreams
and answered their questions.

The kings of Babylon liked Daniel very much
because he helped them rule.
But there came a time
when some of the king's servants
grew jealous of Daniel.
They were afraid that he might become
as powerful as the king.
They wanted to get rid of him,
so they came up with a plan.

In Babylon, people were allowed
to bow down and pray only to the king,
not to anyone else. This was a new law.
The evil ministers saw Daniel bow down
and pray to his God.
They reported this to the king.
Then the king had to punish Daniel.

The king was sad as he said,
"Daniel, you have always been such a help to me.
Now you have broken the law
by bowing down to your God.
Although it pains me greatly to do this,
I must send you to the lion's den.
I only hope your God will save you."

Daniel spent the night
in the lion's den
saying תְּפִלּוֹת t'fillot.
The next morning
the king rushed
to find Daniel.
He saw with great joy that
Daniel was still alive.

"Has your God saved you, Daniel?"
asked the king.

"Yes, my Lord," answered Daniel.
"God sent an angel
to shut the lion's mouths
and so I am safe."

The king was very impressed
with the power of Daniel's תְּפִלָּה t'fillah.
He wrote letters to all the kingdoms of the earth.
The letters said,
"I have seen with my own eyes
that the God of Daniel
is the strongest, wisest,
and most just in the universe.

The kingdom of the God of Daniel
will last forever.

"The תּוֹרָה Torah,
the teachings of the Jewish People,
stands like a tree of life in the driest of deserts.
The Torah stands firm and tall,
giving shade and fruits to the earth
and all those who live on it."

Daniel lived for many years after this.
He spoke to God every day with תְּפִלָּה.

ACTIVITIES

1. *To discuss:* Who else used to rule by dreams? Who helped him understand his dreams? Do you think that this is a good way to rule? Why? Why not?

2. *Imagining the desert:* Have you ever been to the desert? Draw or paint a picture of the desert.

3. *Dancing the desert*: This is a dance for at least four people. Have one person be a plant, tree, or animal in the desert. The others should be Sun, Rain, and Wind. Have Sun, Rain, and Wind take turns coming down on the desert and see how different the desert-being feels, depending on what is at work.

4. *Tav and the alef-bet:* The letter ת tav is the final gateway of the alef-bet. Now you have traveled with the Jewish People through all the letters of the alef-bet and all the stories of the Hebrew Bible.

   Can you recite the whole Hebrew alef-bet? Color in the letter chart as you say the names of the letters.

For Parents and Teachers

ALEF

1. **In the Torah there are many names for "God"**; for example, *Elohim* אֱלֹהִים, *Adonai* יְיָ, *El Shaddai* אֵל שַׁדַּי. These names represent different aspects of divinity that come into play during different parts of the Biblical narrative. The kabbalists, Jewish mystics of the twelfth century onward, claimed that every word in the Torah is a name of God. This belief demonstrates the sacred power of words in Judaism. From this it follows that the letters of those words themselves are molecules of the sacred. Each letter has its own personality and significance.

2. **The rabbis wondered why the first letter of the Torah was not also the first letter of the Hebrew alphabet.** There is a legend that answers this question. The legend is known as a midrash, an interpretive story that seeks to fill in a gap, answer a question, or resolve something that jars the reader of the text. There are many collections of midrashim, attempts by the rabbis to answer such questions. The tradition of making midrashim continues right up to the present day as people still wrestle with the text, trying to understand it and make sense of it. As you read this Torah alphabet with your child, listen to his/her questions. The child's mind and the rabbinic mind are very similar.

   According to this legend, all the letters of the alphabet were vying for first place in the Torah. *Elohim* אֱלֹהִים considered them all in turn but found that each letter started at least one word that had bad connotations. For example, *Gimmel* ג, the third letter of the Hebrew alphabet, starts the words *Gadol* גָּדוֹל (Great) and *Gevurah* גְּבוּרָה (Strength), but it also starts *Ganav* גַּנָּב (Thief). Each letter presented itself as the perfect one to begin the Torah, and in each God found imperfection until the letter Bet ב stepped forward. *Bet* ב begins *Brakhah* בְּרָכָה (Blessing), and, that is how *Elohim* אֱלֹהִים chose to begin the Torah. Only the *Alef* א had not yet come forward; it was quiet and humble, not competitive like the others. So *Elohim* declared, "*Alef* א will start the Ten Commandments because it is so modest"; that is "*Anokhi Adonay Eloheycha* יְיָ אֱלֹהֶיךָ אָנֹכִי—I am the Lord, Your God..." (Exodus 20:2)

3. **In the first part of the Creation story, there are two words that begin with *Alef* א and refer to the earth.** The first word, *Aretz* אֶרֶץ, means "earth" in the broadest sense; that is, "land." People refer to *Eretz Yisrael* אֶרֶץ יִשְׂרָאֵל, lit. the land Israel, and sometimes shorten the

phrase by saying *Ha'Aretz* הָאָרֶץ (The Land), meaning the land of Israel, not any other land. One of the major Hebrew newspapers in Israel is called *Ha'Aretz* הָאָרֶץ.

The second word is *Adamah* אֲדָמָה, which literally means "ground" or "soil," the stuff of which the earth is made, the raw material of which Adam was made.

4. **According to the Torah, there are two Creation stories.** The first one, Genesis 1-2:3, states that Adam was created in God's image, male and female (Genesis 1:27). The second version, Genesis 2:4-25, describes how the first woman, Eve, was born from the first man, Adam. One midrash of the rabbis, an interpretation of the first version in which Adam was created male and female, explains that at first Adam had two faces, one male and one female. God then divided Adam into two beings, one male and one female. This suggests a rather contemporary idea; namely, that each human being contains within him/herself masculine and feminine aspects.

BET

5. **If you listen to the way the Torah begins in the Hebrew, you can hear how different the story sounds from the English,** how it is meant to be sung or read out loud: *Bereishit ba-ra Elohim et ha-shamayim v'et ha-aretz* / בְּרֵאשִׁית בָּרָא אֱלֹהִים אֵת הַשָּׁמַיִם וְאֵת הָאָרֶץ / In the beginning, God was creating the heavens and the earth….

6. *Brakhot* בְּרָכוֹת **(Blessings) for different aspects of life abound in Judaism.** The philosopher Maimonides (1135-1204) established three kinds of blessings: 1) those that have to do with the five senses and the appreciation of what they bring in—as before drinking wine or grape juice; before eating bread; on smelling fragrances; on seeing wonders in nature like shooting stars; high mountains; the sunrise; on hearing thunder or good news; on putting on new clothes; 2) those that are said before one performs a mitzvah (one of the 613 commandments), such as lighting candles for Shabbat and holidays, blowing the shofar, etc.; 3) those that are said to thank God or to make a request of God. The first *Jewish Catalog* written by Strassfeld, Strassfeld and Siegel (Philadelphia: Jewish Publication Society, 1973) outlines the types of blessings and how to make them, pp. 150-157). The letter *bet* ב looks like a primitive structure or dwelling place. The kabbalists, Jewish mystics, used the Hebrew letters as objects of meditation. They would picture the way the letter looked or imagine the way it sounded and use that to direct their attention. This is similar to the way the Hindus and Buddhists use mandalas and mantras in their meditations.

For more on Shabbat, the day of rest, read Abraham Joshua Heschel's *The Sabbath: Its Meaning for Modern Man* (New York: Farrar, Straus, and Giroux, 1951). A picture book that focuses on Shabbat for young readers is Raymond A. Zwerin and Audrey Friedman Marcus' *Shabbat Can Be* (New York: U.A.H.C., 1979).

GIMMEL

1. **More on Noah:** Why was Noah chosen, of all the people on earth, to build the ark and be saved?

   Legends abound of the uniqueness of Noah, even at his birth. His eyes actually gave off light when they opened, filling the room. Further, he opened his mouth and began to give thanks to God. His father, Lamekh, son of Methuselah, was frightened and consulted a seer. Lamekh learned that his son was, indeed, special; he learned that God would destroy the entire earth and all its inhabitants with a flood and that Noah and his family would be saved.

   The text says, "Noah was a righteous man and perfect in his generations and he walked with God" (Genesis 6:9). The rabbis differ on the connotation of "righteous" regarding Noah. Some say he was righteous even in a generation of wicked, depraved people, and if he had been surrounded by good, decent people he would have become even more righteous. Others say that he only appeared righteous because, compared to the others of his generation, he was a model being. If he had lived in the time of Abraham, the Patriarch, his "righteousness" would have meant nothing.

   Whichever viewpoint you find more compelling, it is clear that Noah stood out as an individual whose morals and behavior were a cut above the standards of the times.

2. **A Second Creation:** When God draws back the flood and lets the earth live again, God gives Noah and his sons a blessing that sounds familiar: "Be fruitful and multiply and replenish the earth."

   The last time God spoke these words was to Adam and Eve at the time of their creation (Genesis 1:28). This time God vows never to destroy the earth again.

3. **The Rainbow:** The sign of the covenant between God and humanity is the rainbow. Judaism has several such signs: שַׁבָּת *Shabbat* (day of rest), the Exodus from Egypt. *B'rit Milah* מִילָה בְּרִית (ritual circumcision), the Creation.

   With such a growing awareness of the potential destruction of the world at the hands of human beings through carelessness, consumerism, and pollution of air, water, and earth, some people have gone back to the sources in Judaism to discover what wisdom is there concerning the earth's survival.

   Shomrei Adamah שׁוֹמְרֵי אֲדָמָה (Keepers of the Earth) is an organization whose mission is "to inspire environmental awareness and practice among Jews by unlocking the treasure of ancient Jewish ecological wisdom." For more information, write *Shomrei Adamah*, 804 C, 5500 Wissahickon Ave., Philadelphia, PA 19144.

4. *Noahide Laws:* **Noah and Adam represent every man.** They both lived before the enactment of a covenant between God and the Jewish people. Abraham is generally thought of as the first

Jew because he accepted the idea of one God. The covenant with the Jewish people occurred with the giving of the Torah at Mt. Sinai to Moses after the children of Israel had escaped slavery in Egypt.

The Noahide Law consists of seven laws that the rabbis declared to be the absolute minimum moral requirements for every human being. These are: 1) no idolatry, 2) no blasphemy, 3) no bloodshed, 4) no sexual sins, 5) no theft, 6) no eating from a live animal, and 7) the creation of a system of laws.

DALET

1. **Abraham's hospitality is legendary.** He is considered to be the model for the way one should welcome guests into one's home: running to greet them, giving them refreshment, making sure they are comfortable. Abraham even washed the feet of his guests, a gesture that is greatly appreciated in the desert.

   The desert environment, with its scarcity of food, water, and trees or other kinds of shelter, decrees that all who live there should offer whatever they can to travelers. Such kindness can sometimes be a matter of life or death and not just a formality as it is in less harsh environments. In Israel the first thing a host asks you as you step inside the door is, "What would you like to drink?"

   Ethiopian Jews have a saying, "Welcome! My house is the house of Abraham. Please come in." They mean this quite literally. Hospitality is a *mitzvah*, one of the 613 commandments God gave to the children of Israel. Abraham is the model for how to carry out this *mitzvah*.

2. **Who were these three travelers?** The rabbis interpreted a puzzle in the text as follows:

   The Torah says, "And the Eternal appeared to him (Abraham)…as he sat in the tent door in the heat of the day; and he lifted up his eyes and looked, and lo, three men stood over against him…" (Genesis 18:1,2).

   The text states that "the Eternal appeared," and yet when Abraham looked up he saw "three men." The rabbis conclude that the Eternal appeared to Abraham in the guise of three men or three angels. Whoever these three beings were, they were able to make the promise of a son being born to Abraham and Sarah and to carry it out. Surely this is the work of the Eternal and not just an ordinary guest.

3. **Sarah is the first of the four matriarchs.** Three of the four—Sarah, Rebekkah and Rachel— had great difficulty in conceiving children. Sarah is ninety years old and well past childbearing age when she hears the announcement of the birth of a son in a year.

4. **As Abraham exemplifies hospitality and lovingkindness, Sarah exemplifies faith.** At first she doubts the prophecy that a child will be born to her, and she laughs to herself, but the Lord

chides her, saying, "Is anything too difficult for the Lord?" (Genesis 18:12, 14). Then she must suspend her disbelief, for she is afraid that the son will not be born to her unless she does believe in this miracle.

The Midrash illustrates how Sarah's giving birth at such a late age was not only a test of Sarah's faith but also a test for other people as well.

According to the Midrash, Abraham invited many people to the feast he made in honor of Isaac's circumcision. Many people doubted that she had, indeed, given birth to a baby boy, saying that Isaac must be an abandoned baby they had found on the road somewhere. Therefore, God made a miracle happen. Sarah's breasts were filled with enough milk to nurse all the infants present at the feast. This proved beyond a doubt that Sarah had actually given birth to Isaac (Louis Ginzberg, *Legends of the Jews*. Philadelphia: Jewish Publication Society, 1968, Vol. I, pp. 262-263).

The Midrash reveals God's sense of humor. We know that Sarah laughed when she heard that she would be a mother, that her years of bitterness and despair over being childless must have caused her to see the humor in her fate in order to be able to continue believing in God's justice. In choosing to perform this particular miracle, God also laughs. Here was a woman who was never pregnant her whole life until the age of ninety. Suddenly she bears a child, and her breast milk is not only adequate; it is literally overflowing. It is as if God is saying, "You need proof that I can make these wonders happen? Just watch this!"

Sarah needed a high level of faith in order to sit by while her son was up on Mt. Moriah, nearly being sacrificed by Abraham to God. She understands at that time that the fate of her son is inextricably linked to her husband's relationship with God and not to her own. Abraham is the one being tested. Still, Sarah may have had a part in her son's salvation, for the next time we hear of Sarah, she has died. The proximity of two seemingly unrelated events in the Torah usually signifies that they are, indeed, related. Perhaps she gave her life in exchange for her son's, surrendering herself to the will of God. In this case, it is easy to see in Sarah a strength of purpose that caused Abraham to "hearken" to her voice (Genesis 16: 1,2).

HEH

1. **The importance of *Heh* ה can be seen in the name changes that Abram and Sarai underwent.** When God makes a convenant with the first Father and Mother of the Jewish people, God says,

   "Neither shall your name any more be called Abram, but your name shall be Abraham; for a father of many nations have I made you...."

And God said to Abraham, "As for Sarai your wife, you shall not call her name Sarai, but Sarah shall her name be. And I will bless her, and give you a son also of her...and she shall be a mother of nations; kings of peoples shall issue from her" (Genesis 17:5, 15-16).

Abram means "exalted father," and *Abraham* means "father of a multitude." *Sarai* means "my princess," and *Sarah* means "princess." The *Heh* ה magnifies the greatness of the first Mother and Father of the Jewish people.

2. **Child Brides:** According to the Midrash, Rebekkah was a very young girl when she met Eliezer at the well. She may even have been as young as three. This is not as dire as it sounds. In Ethiopia, until very recently, when most of the Jews emigrated to Israel, it was still quite common for girls to be "married" as early as eight or nine years old. They would leave their own family and go to live with her husband's family. The girl did not actually cohabit with her husband until she reached the age of menarche. Even then, she and her husband lived with his family for many years, until he was economically independent. The young bride was under the protection and care of his parents. This was a great financial burden off her parents. The responsibility for numerous children (as many as the mother could produce in her lifetime) weighed heavily on parents, and child brides were quite common. This changed when the Ethiopian Jews came to Israel.

    See Winn-Lederer, Ilene, *Kind Little Rivka*. Brooklyn, N.Y.: HaChai Publishing, 1991.

3. **It is interesting to note that the blessing Rebekkah's family gave her when she left to marry Isaac is the same blessing used in traditional Jewish wedding ceremonies today.**

    "And they (her brother and her mother)
    blessed Rebekkah, and said to her,
    You are our sister, be you the mother
    of thousands and ten thousands..." (Genesis 24:60).

4. **Other Words Beginning with *Heh* ה:**

    Har הָר (Mountain)

    Hadassah הֲדַסָּה (hebrew name of Esther, lit. myrtle)

    Halakhah הֲלָכָה (lit. walking, the way; the way of carrying out the *mitzvot*)

VAV

1. **Rebekkah actually talks to God in this story.** The Torah says that she went to "inquire of God" as to why there was such a ruckus in her womb. God answers her as stated previously. From this it is possible to conclude that Rebekkah was indeed a prophetess; that is, she was able to communicate directly with God. According to the rabbis, there were seven

prophetesses—Tamar, Miram, Hannah, Abigail, Bat-Sheva, Deborah and Huldah—in addition to the four Matriarchs, who were, of course, also prophetesses in their own right.

Sarah knew that her son Isaac would be one of the foundations of the Jewish people, which was why God told Abraham to listen to Sarah and to cast out Hagar and Ishmael.

Rebekkah possessed the prophetic powers listed above.

Rachel and Leah named their sons in ways that indicated they knew what the future would bring. For example, according to the Midrash, Rachel named her first son "Joseph," which means "Increase" in Hebrew. The reason she gave for naming him thus was "the Lord will add to me another son" (Genesis 30:24).

2. **The letter *Vav* ו denotes the number six in Hebrew.** *Vav* ו signifies completion. The world was created in six days. *Vav* ו is also significant in the transformation of the Jewish people from a nation of slaves to a nation of free beings. There were 600,000 people present at Sinai, and there are just as many letters in the Torah (Maharal as cited in Rabbi Michael L. Munk, *The Wisdom in the Hebrew Alphabet*. New York: Mesorah Publications, Ltd., 1983, p. 94a).

3. **In this story of the importance of the birthright, the power of words is clear.** If spoken with the proper intention and focus, words have tremendous potential. Thus, Isaac was not able to take back the words of the blessing for the firstborn he had given, even though under false pretenses, to his younger son, Jacob.

4. **In the prayerbook, one of the prayers for the Shabbat morning service begins, *Barukh sh'amar v'haya ha'olam* בָּרוּךְ שֶׁאָמַר וְהָיָה הָעוֹלָם (Blessed is the One Who spoke and the world came into being).** This describes the Jewish view of the potent force inherent in words.

ZAYIN

1. **"Surely the Eternal is in this place and I did not know" (Genesis 28:16).** This is what Jacob says after he has the dream of the ladder during which God speaks to him directly. This is the first time Jacob seems to recognize that he, too, is able to have an intimate relationship with God, just as his father did, and just as his father did before him.

2. An entire book has been written recently, a midrash on this one line. The book is called *God Was in This Place and I, I Did not know*, written by Rabbi Lawrence Kushner (Vermont: Jewish Lights Publishing, 1992).

3. Legend has it that God intended for Jacob to stay one night on the site of the future Holy Temple. Indeed, when Jacob awoke from his dream, he observed. "This is Beth-El (the House of God)." He then anointed the rock. God took this same rock and sank it deep down into the center of the earth, where it became the foundation stone of the Holy Temple. The name of God was inscribed on it (Ginzberg, Legends, Vol. I: 352).

Other *Zayin* ז (Words)

- *Zakhar* זָכַר (remembrance, as in *Yizkor* יִזְכּוֹר, special prayer service for the remembrance of the dead)

- *Zayit* זַיִת (Olive)

- *Zaken* זָקֵן (Beard, old person)

- *Zarah* זָרַח (Rising of the sun; hence *Mizrah* East, the symbol placed on the Eastern wall of the synagogue and home to indicate the direction of Jerusalem)

<u>HET</u>

1. **Two Sisters.** The theme of two sisters competing for the same man occurs frequently in literature and folklore. A recent book, *Like Water for Chocolate,* by Laura Esquivel exemplifies this story, as does Shakespeare's *The Taming of the Shrew.*

   The appearances of the two sisters are always in contrast to each other. The beautiful one is younger; the plain one is older. The older must be married first, and this is the central difficulty around which the story revolves. In the case of Leah, all the text says about her looks is "Leah's eyes were weak." In recent times, when the tendency to explore the heretofore silent women's voices in the Torah is strong, Jewish women writers have focused on Leah as well as on the relationship between Rachel and Leah. See Rivka Miriam's poem giving voice to Leah, "A Song to Jacob Who Removed the Stone from the Mouth of the Well," in *Four Centuries of Jewish Women's Spirituality,* edited by E. Umansky and D. Ashton, p. 226 (Boston: Beacon Press, 1992).

   Also, see Rabbi Ruth Sohn's midrash on the ongoing struggle between Rachel and Leah in *Taking the Fruit: Modern Women's Tales of the Bible* (San Diego Woman's Institute for Continuing Jewish Education, 1989, pp. 61-64).

2. **Malls and Wells.** Wells appear quite often in the Torah. This is not surprising as water is a prime commodity for every desert people. Meetings at a well have a connotation similar to that of meetings today at the mall. The mall is merely a contemporary "watering place" where people go to replenish their supplies. In the Torah there is a deeper significance, as the Torah itself is considered to be a source of "spiritual" water for those who are wandering in their own deserts.

   Consider all the crucial meetings that took place at the well: Rebekkah met Eliezer, emissary for Isaac, her intended; Rachel met Jacob; Tzipporah met Moses (Exodus 2:15-21).

3. **Other Words that Begin with *Het* ח:** Hanukkah חֲנֻכָּה (Festival of Lights)

   Het חַטְא (Sin), as in *Avinu Malkeinu, Hatanu v'Ashamnu* (Our Father, Our King, We have sinned and we have been guilty) prayer from Yom Kippur liturgy.

4. **Het** ח**, the Eighth Letter.** The number eight figures in circumcision, which happens on the eighth day of a baby boy's life. Also, there are eight days of Pesah, eight days of Sukkot, and eight days of חֲנֻכָּה Hanukkah. Eight means completion and then some. The world was created in six days, culminating in a seventh day of rest. Jacob fulfilled a "week" of years (Genesis 29:27), seven to be exact, in order to marry Rachel. But this was not enough. He had to work for Laban an additional seven years before he could actually marry her. Seven and then some before his soul was completed through his beloved Rachel.

TET

1. **The first Tet** ט **in the Torah occurs in the word Tov** טוֹב**. "And God said, Let there be light and there was light. And God saw the light, that it was good…" (Genesis 1:3).**

   According to the Rabbis, this gives the letter *Tet* ט a very positive connotation, a significance full of "goodness."

2. **In Hebrew, the letters Tet** ט **and Tav** ת **represent the sound "T." However, in Ashkenazic (Eastern European) Jewish pronunciation of Hebrew, the Tav** ת **often sounds like an "S."** The *Tet* ט sound is made by lightly touching the tip of the tongue to the back of the teeth, while the *Tav* ת sound is made by pressing the tongue further back against the roof of the mouth, which makes the "ts" sound.

3. **Joseph sounds the call for a paradigm shift.** While life had been conducted through a nomadic shepherd model, he reasoned that in an era of scarce resources (famine and drought) it made more sense for his people to cluster around cities, where there was steady work and pay. His brothers and father balked at this idea, foreshadowed in dreams in which they all bow down to him. But Joseph's idea won out in the end when the Jewish people migrated down to Egypt, becoming merchants and city dwellers themselves. (I am grateful to Rabbi Gershon Siegel of Newton, MA, for these ideas.)

4. **Other words beginning with Tet** ט: *Tut* טוט is sound of a shofar; *Treif* טְרֵף (non-kosher) from the root *Tet-Reish-Fey* [טרף] (tear in pieces, wound, injure). In the story about Joseph that the brothers tell their father, Jacob must assume that something terrible has happened to his favorite son. He beholds the coat of many colors he had given his son with such love. The coat has been dipped in blood so that it will appear that Joseph has met a violent end. When Jacob sees the coat, he says, "This is my son's coat; an evil beast has devoured him; Joseph is certainly *Taraf* טָרֹף (torn to pieces)."

YUD

1. **The Hand of God and the Eye of God are two concepts that are quite prevalent in Jewish thought.** The letter *Yud* י signifies both. The *Yud* י is related to the word *Yad* יָד meaning "hand," and the shape of the *Yud* י has been connected to the eye.

   There is a good luck symbol used all over the Middle East called a ḥamsa. It is a stylized hand made from many sorts of decorative materials—gold, silver, brass, cloth, paper. Often there is a single eye placed in the center of it. The purpose of the ḥamsa is protection of the house where it is posted or the person who is wearing it. The Eye of God within the Hand of God. Both the eye and the hand are aspects of the letter *Yud* י.

2. **The *Yud* י signifies humility because of its size.** It is actually the smallest letter in the Hebrew alphabet. Munk states (p. 126) that *Yud* י stands for the essence, what remains after all else has been removed.

3. ***Yud* י also stands for God.** Two *Yuds* יְי together and *Yud-Heh-Vav-Heh* יהוה are both names of God, read as *Adonai*, literally "My Lord." The first time *Yud-Heh-Vav-Heh*, the Tetragrammaton, appears in the Torah is in Exodus 3:15. God responds to Moses's questions, "Who shall I say has sent me when the children of Israel ask, What is the name of the God of our Fathers? What shall I say to them?" by saying, "Tell them that *Yud-Heh-Vav-Heh*, the God of your Fathers, the God of Abraham, the God of Isaac, and the God of Jacob, has sent you."

   The Tetragrammaton comes from the root meaning "to be." What the four letters signify is the essence of being. The *Yud*, the essential letter, initiates the Tetragrammaton.

Other *Yud* י words: *Yisrael* יִשְׂרָאֵל (Israel); *Ya'akov* יַעֲקֹב (Jacob); *Yitzhak* יִצְחָק (Isaac); *Yam* יָם (Sea); *Yamin* יָמִין (Right-hand); *Yafa* יָפָה (Girl's name meaning "beautiful"); *Yayin* יַיִן (Wine).

KAF

1. **Famine has been seen, throughout the world, as a sign of the breakdown of the relationship between God and humanity, as a sign of wrongdoing on the part of mortal beings.** In Jewish liturgy we read again and again how there is a contract between God and us. If we do God's commandments and lead lives according to the Torah, God will make the earth bring forth fruit at the proper time, and all will be well. One could understand the state of the earth and the environment today in these terms. *Shomrei ha-Adamah* (Keepers of the Earth) is an organization formed to educate people as to what the Jewish tradition has to say about the environment and what the Jewish community can do about this. See Gimmel, note 3.

Famine is one such sign of the deterioration of the contract between God and humanity. There are ten famines brought by God upon the world as punishment, according to the Midrash. The first came as a result of the sin of Adam and Eve, when God cursed the ground. The second occurred during Abraham's lifetime. The third happened during the time of Isaac and forced him to settle in the land of the Philistines. The fourth was the famine that forced Joseph's brothers to come to Egypt, seeking food. The fifth is cited at the start of the Book of Ruth. The sixth happened while King David ruled. The seventh occurred in the Prophet Elijah's time. The eighth happened when Elisha lived. The ninth comes even today, in different places, all over the world. The tenth sounds uncannily present now. It is the one that signals the coming of the Messiah; that is, the famine of hearing the words of God (Ginzberg, Legends, Vol. I:220-221).

2. *Kaf* כ **Closed and Open**: At Havdalah, the ritual marking the end of Shabbat, there is a custom that has to do with starting to use lights again. During the entire Shabbat it is not permissible, among observant Jews, to light fires. As the Havdalah candle is lit we hold our hands up to the light, using it to see them by. It is customary to open and close the hands several times by the light of this candle. The open and relaxed hand denotes Shabbat rest and peace. The tightly closed hand represents the beginning of the week of acquiring and doing now that Shabbat is over (Maharam Rothenburg in Munk, p. 135).

Other *Kaf* כ Words: *Kotel* כֹּתֶל (Western Wall of Solomon's Temple in Jerusalem; often referred to as the Wailing Wall); *Kisseh* כְּסֵא (Throne; Chair); *Kos* כּוֹס (Cup); *Kasher* כָּשֵׁר (Kosher; in accordance with Jewish dietary laws).

LAMED

1. **Learning is a major Jewish value.** Even in homes where there is not much ritual observance, the presence of books and the emphasis on serious study reveals the primacy of learning.

There is a midrash that says that Mt. Sinai was the location of the first yeshiva or Jewish learning center. Moses taught Torah to the Jewish people at the foot of the mountain so they could understand what God wanted of them.

But even more than this, the act of study, in a Jewish context, is a sacred act, a way of connecting with God and the community of learners, a way of understanding the meaning of existence. The notion of study for its own sake (*Torah l'Shmah*) is crucial in Judaism. It signifies that the process of study supersedes the acquisition of knowledge. What is it about the process that allows this to happen?

First of all, in traditional Jewish learning contexts, people study in groups, with or without a teacher. Or they study with a partner. This ensures that one does not become so cut off from the rest of the community that s/he sees the text through one lens only. The rabbis knew how dangerous this could be.

Second, when one studies for the sake of study alone, s/he is able to enter into the text, identifying with key figures, understanding their struggles, victories, and losses. One forms a bond with the ancestors. Sociologist Samuel Heilman has studied Jewish learning quite closely in his two books, *Synagogue Life* (Chicago: University of Chicago Press, 1973) and *The People of the Book* (Chicago: University of Chicago Press, 1987).

Finally, in *Pirkei Avot: Sayings of the Fathers*, Rabbi Meir enumerates the rewards for one who studies Torah for its own sake:

"Rabbi Meir said, Whosoever labors in the Torah for its own sake, merits many things; and not only so, but the whole world is indebted to him: he is called friend, beloved, a lover of the All-present, a lover of mankind; it clothes him in meekness and reverence…it keeps him far from sin and brings him near to virtue…to him the secrets of the Torah are revealed; he is made like a never-failing fountain…

2. **The Hebrew midwives may be responsible for the salvation of the Jewish people. By their acts of quiet resistance they made sure that Pharaoh's evil decree to kill all male babies would not go into effect.** They stood up to Pharaoh, saying that even before they could reach the Hebrew women, they had already given birth.

Miriam and her mother were the midwives mentioned in the text (Exodus 1:15), according to the Midrash. They went by the names Shifrah and Puah. Miram revealed her prophetic powers at a young age. She was able to see that her newborn brother, Moses, would be a great leader of the Jewish people even before he was born. Miriam convinced her father to resume conjugal relations with her mother. He had separated himself from his wife because he did not want to bring any more children into the jaws of slavery. On hearing Miriam's prophecy he went back to his wife, and Moses was born.

Thus Miram was a "spiritual midwife" as well, coaxing her people into nationhood step by step through her prophetic and persuasive abilities.

Levi is the name of one of the twelve tribes of Israel. The others are Reuben, Judah, Dan, Asher, Shimeon, Yissachar, Naphtali, Joseph, Zevulun, Gad, and Benjamin. The Levites were the priestly class. They performed ritual acts of purification and service to God on behalf of the entire community. Moses, Miriam and Aaron were, therefore, heirs to a sacred tradition of being close to God, understanding the divine will and being able to convey it to the people.

MEM

1. **The following familiar midrash could be an answer to question #4.**

   Pharaoh's advisers were very suspicious when they beheld the new baby that the princess had rescued. They put the idea into Pharaoh's head that Moses might someday take over as ruler.

   Pharaoh believed his advisers and decided to test the baby. He would put two glittering objects before the baby: some hot coals and the crown. If the baby reached out for the crown, then he must be banished from the kingdom. If the baby reached for the hot coals, however, it was clear that he simply liked shiny things and posed no real threat to Pharaoh.

   The test was carried out. Moses was about to reach for the crown when an angel guided his hand to the coals. Moses touched one of the hot coals to his mouth and was saved from banishment. However, he burned his tongue, and from that time on he had difficulty speaking.

2. **Another midrash stresses the goodness of Pharaoh's daughter and how she was assisted by God in rescuing Moses.** According to this midrash, the princess reached out to take the baby from the ark, but her arm was not long enough. Just then an angel came and extended her arm so that she could easily reach the baby. This presages the "outstretched arm" of God that delivered the Israelites from Egypt.

3. **It is no accident that the same word in Hebrew is used for the basket of Moses and the boat of Noah.** Noah's arks preserved enough humans and animals to initiate a new world, and Moses' ark preserved the future redeemer of the Jewish people.

4. **The name Moshe in Hebrew actually means "one who draws out" as opposed to "drawn out,"** which Pharaoh's daughter gives as the translation. Why would the text contain such a discrepancy? The rabbis contend that the name could be prophetic in that Moses would eventually be the "one who draws out" the children of Israel from Egypt.

5. **More *Mem* מ words:** *Matzah* מַצָּה and *Mayim* מַיִם (water).

6. **Other letters that have beginning and final forms like the *Mem* מ are:** *Kaf* כ; *Nun* נ; *Peh* פ; and *Tzadi* צ.

NUN

1. **In the King James Version of the Bible, it is referred to as the Red Sea.** This is a misnomer. In Hebrew, this body of water is known as *Yam Suf* יָם סוּף (lit. Sea of Reeds and Reed Sea) because of the distinctive vegetation growing around it. This became mistakenly known as the Red Sea. There is nothing red about the sea at all.

2. **According to the Midrash, there is another test of Moses' faith God made even before the burning bush.**

   Moses was tending his sheep when he noticed that one had wandered away from the rest of the flock. He sought it out and found it drinking at a nearby stream.

   "I didn't know you were so thirsty, poor lamb. Drink your fill and come back with me to the rest of the flock."

   God said to Moses, "Because you have taken the time to go after one in your care who has wandered away from the rest, I have confidence in you to take care of my flock, the People Israel. Someday you are going to need the same patience and understanding you have shown today with this little thirsty creature, and I know that I will be able to count on you."

3. **Has there been a "burning bush" in your life—a time when you felt a sacred presence?** What was this like? Share this with your child, if you can.

4. **In the Torah (Exodus 15:1-19; 20-21) there are two versions of the Song of the Sea, verses that celebrate the safe crossing of the children of Israel.** The first version is sung by Moses and the children of Israel. The second version is sung by Miriam and danced by the women. However, this second version is only a fragment of the first. Miriam utters only the first verse of her brother's version and that is all.

   This enticing fragment of Miriam's gave rise to the midrash about the Song of Sea. The Rabbis were intrigued by the unfinished character of Miriam's version of the Song. Why was Miriam's version incomplete and Moses's version complete?

   The answer the Rabbis gave demonstrates a sensitivity to future generations. The incompleteness of Miriam's version makes it incumbent on each succeeding generation to finish the song. This has a parallel in the Passover Haggadah, where it says, "In every generation, it is the obligation of each and every person to see him/herself as if s/he has personally come out of Egypt."

SAMEKH

1. *Torah m'Sinai* תּוֹרָה מִסִּינַי. One of the central tenets separating the different Jewish denominations is the concept of *Torah m'sinai* or Torah from Sinai. What does this mean?

   Simply put, some Jews believe that the Torah was received by Moses up on Mount Sinai directly from God. In effect, this means that the Torah is the "word of God," and all the commandments in it are from a divine source and must be obeyed because of their source.

   Other Jews believe that while Moses was up on the mountain for forty days he became divinely inspired to write the Torah himself. Thus, while Moses may have been touched by a divine spark, he ultimately was responsible for everything in the Torah—stories, laws, explanations.

   The legend that states that the entire Jewish people, even those who had already died and those who were yet unborn, was present at Sinai demonstrates what a pivotal event this was. It implies that whatever your belief, that whether the Torah is from a divine source or a human source, the events at Sinai changed the Jewish people forever. This legend also points to the underlying unity of the Jewish people. If we were all at Sinai, then we all witnessed the central event that determined the course of Jewish history and Judaism.

2. **There is a saying, "There is no 'before' or 'after' in the Torah."** All events happen simultaneously on the cosmic timeline. We who are living in the 20th century C.E. are no farther from Sinai than those who were alive the year it happened.

3. **Other *Samekh* ס Words:** *Siddur* סִדּוּר (Prayerbook); *Seder* סֵדֶר (literally order; the ritual Passover meal); *Sabba* סַבָּא (grandfather); *Savta* סַבְתָּא (grandmother).

AYIN

1. **The true sound of *Ayin* ע.** Ayin is pronounced with a glottal stop. This is made by pressing your tongue against your throat and saying Ayin-Ayin-Ayin. Do you hear something that sounds like a bottle being emptied? That is the glottal stop, almost a "gh-gh-gh" sound. That's why the *Azah* עַזָה Strip is pronounced Gaza in English. The Yemenite Jews are among the few groups that pronounce *Ayin* ע correctly today.

2. ***Shabbat*, Today's Holy Temple.** Ever since the Temple was destroyed, certain of its elements found their way into the home. On Shabbat we light candles to remind us of the sacred fire that consecrated the Temple. The two loaves of challah symbolize the sacrifices offered in the Temple; hence the salting of the bread. The table itself where we eat our special Shabbat meals represents the altar upon which the sacrifices were offered (see Exodus 26:35).

3. **The Eye of the World.** There is a midrash that likens the world with Jerusalem at the center to the eye of a human being. The white of the eye is all the oceans and seas. The dark part is the world. The darkest part in the center is Jerusalem. And in the center of that is the Holy Temple. (See Ze'ev Vilnay, *Stories of the Land of Israel.* Jerusalem: Kiriat Sefer, 1950 (Hebrew); Transl. into English as *Legends of the Sacred Land*, Philadelphia: Jewish Publication Society, 1973-1978.)

The story goes that everybody wanted to contribute something to the making of the Holy Temple, but when the women tried to contribute their mirrors, Moses refused their offering. He did not want anything in the sanctuary that might stir up lust and desire.

However, God said to him, "These mirrors are very precious to me. With these mirrors the women gazed at themselves and made themselves beautiful for their husbands. The men lost all hope as slaves and stopped caring about having any sexual relations with their wives. But the women kept them interested enough by virtue of the mirrors so that they resumed relations and had many children together. These mirrors have kept the people of Israel alive."

So Moses accepted the gift of the women and used the mirrors to make the vessel containing the water used to consecrate the priests (Ginzberg, *Legends*, Vol. III: pp. 174-175).

PEH

1. **Besides embodying the essence of what individual prayer is about, Hannah also was seen by the rabbis to be the model for the fulfillment of commandments incumbent upon women.** There are three, according to traditional Judaism. They are *Hallah* (taking a portion of the dough and burning it as a symbolic sacrifice to God); *Niddah* (ritual separation of wife and husband while the woman is menstruating); and *Hadlakat Nerot* (lighting Shabbat candles). Hannah's name is an acronym of the initial letters—*Het-Nun-Heh* חנה.

   Infertility is a major theme among the Mothers in the Torah. Sarah, Rebekkah, Rachel, and Hannah all demonstrated their steadfast belief in God through their childbearing trials. Hannah's deep faith in God is also put to the test as she prays and waits for a child.

   See Michael Gold, *And Hannah Wept* (Philadelphia: Jewish Publication Society, 1988), and the author's "The Womb and the Word" in E. Umansky and D. Ashton, *Four Centuries of Jewish Women's Spirituality* (Beacon Press, 1992), pp. 247-257.

2. **This story echoes a theme in the midrashim about Hannah and Peninah.** One midrash says that Peninah used to taunt Hannah because she could not have children and yet was still more beloved by Elkanah. This kind of speech was in direct contrast to Hannah's "sacred" speech in the Temple, where her words come from her heart and serve to transform her from a barren woman to a fertile one.

A Comparison Tale: Diamonds and Snakes in *The Blue Fairy Book*, The Brothers Grimm

Once there were two sisters. One was good and beautiful, and one was wicked and quite plain. The mother favored the plain one and used to make the beautiful sister do most of the work around the house.

One day the mother sent her into the woods to fetch a pail of water from the well. The day was hot, the sun was high, but she did not complain as she set off with the bucket on her head. When she arrived at the well there was a poor old woman who begged her for a cup of water. The girl helped her gladly, filled her bucket, and went on her way back home.

When she returned home, what a surprise! Her mother asked what took her so long. "I met an old woman and—". Suddenly a diamond and two roses popped out of her mouth. Every few words, more jewels and flowers came. Her mother figured out that the old woman must be responsible for this wonderful spell. She immediately ordered the other girl to get a bucket and go quickly to the well.

"Oh, do I have to?" whined the girl. Her mother shooed her out the door.

Sure enough, she also met up with a stranger at the well. This one was young, though, and riding a white horse. She asked the girl if she might have a drink, and the girl rudely replied, "Why should I get it for you? What am I—your servant?"

The girl returned home. As soon as she opened her mouth to speak, snakes and vipers leaped out. She was horrified, as was her mother. She remained inside the house for the rest of her days, while her sister married a prince and lived in the palace.

3. **Other *Peh* פ words:** *Purim* פּוּרִים (Feast of Lots, which takes place in early spring); *Pesah* פֶּסַח (Passover); *Pazzazz* "פַּזַז" (Pizzazz); *Panim* פָּנִים (Face).

TZADI

1. **The *Tzadik* or *Tzadeket* is an important figure in Jewish lore and literature.** Among the Hasidim there are many tales of *Tzadikim*. In fact, the Baal Shem Tov, the founder of Hasidism, was one of the greatest *Tzadikim*. Tales of his goodness and wisdom abound (See Dan Ben-Amos and Jerome R. Mintz, *In Praise of the Baal Shem Tov*. Bloomington, Indiana: Indiana University Press, 1970).

2. **One aspect of this kind of person is hiddenness.** The sign of a true *Tzadik* is that s/he never reveals him/herself. Rather, s/he performs the righteous act unobtrusively, without fanfare. The same is true of *Tzedakah*. The highest form of giving is anonymous giving.

Among the Sephardic Jews, there are many *Tzadikim* in this day and age who have the power to heal, to prophesy, to bless.

3. **Shavuot (Feast of Weeks) is the culmination of the seven-week period commencing with Pesa<u>h</u> in early Spring.** The day after Pesa<u>h</u>, the *omer* or grain offering was brought to the Temple. Then it was time to start marking off forty-nine days until *Shavuot*. After this initial offering was brought, it was permitted to partake of the harvest.

4. **Why do we read the Book of Ruth on Shavuot?** Ruth, a stranger to the Jewish People and the first "convert," according to the Rabbis, was the great-grandmother of King David. In a sense, all those present at Sinai became "converts" to the form of Judaism Moses conveyed from a divine source. In her natural acceptance of the Torah through Naomi, Ruth is a model for receiving the Torah with complete faith and trust.

KUF

1. **Most of the Psalms in the Hebrew Bible are attributed to King David.** They often start out with the formula, "A Song of David." The well-known Psalm 3 is one of these: "A Song of David. The Lord is my shepherd; I shall not lack anything…"

2. The story of David and Goliath is a quintessential "Jewish" story. That is, Jewish history is full of episodes when the Jewish people were the underdogs, the less powerful, and yet they overcame the odds and came out on top. Even today the survival of the modern state of Israel against odds that seem insurmountable is often compared to David, who took on a giant and won.

3. **A Comparison Tale.** There are many stories that prove that smaller often means braver, wiser, and more clever. Aesop's fable, The Lion and the Mouse, is an example.

The Lion and the Mouse

Once there was a mouse who scampered across a lion's back while it was sleeping. The lion awoke and was about to devour the mouse when the little creature pleaded, "Please, oh, please, mighty lion, spare me. I only thought you were a mound of earth, which is why I scampered over your back. If you let me go today, I will repay you someday."

The lion laughed at the thought of the mouse being able to help him in any way at all. "Very well, little creature. I'll let you go this once, but I'd like to know how you could ever hope to repay me."

The mouse thanked the lion many times. "I know I'll be able to repay you one day. You'll see." And the mouse ran away.

Several weeks later the mouse heard a terrible roaring in the forest. He ran to see what it was. The lion who had spared him was caught in a net.

The mouse jumped onto the net and started biting away at it with his teeth. Soon the lion was free.

"I should have known," said the lion. "You're the mouse who vowed to help me if ever there was a need. You certainly saved my life today. I will never forget this."

The lion and the mouse were friends for the rest of their lives.

4. **Other *Kuf* ק Words**: *K'dushah* קְדוּשָׁה (Holiness, Sacredness); *Kiddush* קִדּוּשׁ (Blessing over wine said on Shabbat and holidays); *Kaddish* קַדִּישׁ (Prayer of praise for God said in honor of a person who has died); *K'dushah* קְדוּשָׁה (Sacredness), a fundamental concept in Judaism. Essentially every act of a human being performs, from going to the bathroom to blessing the matzah at the Pesah seder, from seeing a rainbow to witnessing a death, is full of *K'dushah*. By making blessings and saying prayers, one is acknowledging the presence of the divine in all aspects of life.

For more on this see Strassfeld, Strassfeld, and Siegel, *The Jewish Catalog* (Philadelphia: JPS, 1973).

Also see Blu Greenberg, *How to Run a Traditional Jewish Household* (New York: Simon and Schuster, 1983).

RESH

1. **The Author King. Besides being a great king, Solomon was an accomplished writer.** The Song of Songs, the Book of Proverbs, and Ecclesiastes are all attributed to him. He is deemed to have written these works in his youth, his middle years, and his old age, respectively.

2. **Solomon's Temple.** King Solomon also built the First Holy Temple in Jerusalem. Today, if you go to the Old City of Jerusalem to see the Western Wall of the Temple, you will be standing in front of all that remains standing of the original structure built by Solomon.

3. **The Riddles of a Queen.** There are many legends about King Solomon. Some of them have to do with the beautiful and clever Queen of Sheba, the land that we call Ethiopia today.

All over the world people had heard of King Solomon, the wise and just ruler who always had an answer for every question, every problem. People came from far and wide to seek his advice.

Once the gorgeous Queen of Sheba came to test Solomon's wisdom. She asked him many riddles, such as: Which land has seen the sun only once? (Answer: the bed of the Reed Sea on the day it was divided.)

What was not yet born, yet life was given to it? (Answer: the Golden Calf.)

Solomon answered all of the riddles. The Queen of Sheba was very impressed. "You have the wisest *Rosh* ראש (Head) I have ever known," she told him. The King and Queen fell in love. As one version of the story goes, the royal pair married and had a son, Menelik, who was the ancestor of the Ethiopian Jews today.

(The account of the Queen of Sheba's visit to King Solomon is given in First Kings 10:1-13. The actual riddles are listed in Ginzberg's *Legends,* Vol. IV: 145-149. The story of the marriage of the Queen and King is part of the folklore of Ethiopian Jews.)

SHIN

1. **Purim Memories:** What do you remember of Purim as a child? Did you attend a carnival, bake hamentashen, see a Purimshpiel? Share these memories with the child to whom you are reading.

2. **Anti-Semitism.** This is a good time for a discussion of anti-Semitism. You may want to frame the discussion in a more general way at first, depending on the age of the child. Anti-Semitism is another example of fear of difference. Some people are afraid of whatever is strange or different: people of color, Jews, people with disabilities, or immigrants. Some people single out one of these groups to fear and dislike intensely.

3. **Resources:** Peter Speier, *People* (Garden City, NY: Doubleday and Company, 1980). Contact the Anti-Defamation League in your city for their catalog called "A World of Difference" on educational materials for multicultural education.

4. **More Purim Lore:** Esther's mother died at her birth and her father had died shortly before, so her Uncle Mordecai and his wife took care of her. Mordecai did not think himself above doing things for the baby that were usually done by women.

5. **Esther's other name was Hadass or Myrtle.** Like the plant, she was lovely to behold, but inside there was a pungency, an intensity that enabled her to come to the aid of her people in time of crisis. Also like the myrtle flower, whose perfume spreads far and wide, news of Hadass' good deeds traveled quite a distance.

6. **"Esther" means "hidden."** Mordecai tried to hide his niece, to protect her from King Ahashueros' search for a new queen. However, word of her great beauty came out, and she had to participate in the beauty contest like all the other maidens in the land. Esther is sometimes called the Moon of Israel, for, like the moon, she appeared in Israel's darkest hour to shed light on a dire situation.

TAV

1. **Oral and Written Torah:** The Torah consists of Genesis, Exodus, Leviticus, Numbers, and Deuteronomy. These are also called The Five Books of Moses because they are believed to be the very words Moses received from God on Mt. Sinai. (See Chapter Fifteen: *Samekh* ס on the meaning of "Torah from Sinai.") These books are also known as The Written Law.

   Moses began to teach his first *Torah* תּוֹרָה class at Mount Sinai to the newly freed slaves: men and women, old and young, faithful ones and doubting ones. The Torah was more than just the Written Law, however. The explanations and teachings of Moses about the sacred text are contained in the Oral Torah, compiled by later generations into the Mishnah and Gemara. It is the task of every generation to understand the Torah anew, to find the truths in it that must be passed down to the next generation, to transform the ancient words and meanings into usable guideposts for living today.

2. **The story of Daniel takes place in approximately the sixth century BCE.** This is prior to Queen Esther's period. However, in the Hebrew Bible, Daniel comes after Esther. There is a link between the two stories in that Daniel was said to have been buried in Shushan, the location of Esther's court.

3. **According to legend, the location of Daniel's grave became a bone of contention in Shushan, for he was buried next to a river that divided the city between rich and poor.** He was first buried on the side of more wealth. However, the poor people contended that if he was buried on their side, this might bring more wealth into their neighborhoods.

   Finally, the king placed the bier on a chain that hung above the middle of the river. He also built a synagogue there above the water and forbade fishing for a mile on either side of the tomb. When people who were not God-fearing went by the spot, they would drown. Those who were God-fearing passed by unharmed. The fish that swam beneath the spot were said to have heads shining like gold.

4. **This is a good time to review all the letters and stories together.** See if you can remember which letters represent which stories. Try to remember the Hebrew words you learned, for they are the keys to remembering the stories. This is much the way the Oral Law works. There are certain key words that occur throughout the particular Mishnah or Gemara being studied. By remembering these words, one remembers the main points of the section.

   A fellow student in Jerusalem named Alan Rabinowitz who was studying at the same place I was remarked that a key word is like a magnifying glass. By using it to focus on the larger many-worded text, one is able to remember key points of the text without consciously memorizing.